Polly Marchant

M000035801

# MACHINE KNITTING
## The Technique of
# Slipstitch

## DENISE MUSK

# MACHINE KNITTING
## The Technique of
# Slipstitch

## DENISE MUSK

B.T. Batsford Ltd

© Denise Musk 1989
First published 1989
Reprinted 1989 (twice)

All rights reserved. No part of this publication may be reproduced in any form
or by any means, without permission from the Publisher

ISBN 0 7134 5632 9

Typeset by Servis Filmsetting Ltd, Manchester
and printed in Great Britain by
Butler & Tanner, Frome, Somerset
for the publishers
B.T. Batsford Ltd
4 Fitzhardinge Street
London W1H 0AH

Illustrations by Janet Poole
Photographs by Warwick Dickinson

*To Kathleen Kinder for all her guidance and encouragement given over the years.*

*To Roger my husband, and Adele my daughter, for their help and understanding over the last two years.*

# Acknowledgements

My thanks to Glenda McNicholas and Adele Musk for helping to type the script, to Janet Poole for the illustrations and to Warwick Dickinson for the photography. I am indebted to Shirley Gaskin, the editor of *Australian Machine Knitters Magazine*, for permission to refer to articles and punchcards in past issues of the magazine. Thanks are also due to Jackie Marklew, Jones & Brother, and to Jean Wiseman, Knitmaster, for allowing me access to their electronic knitting machines.

# Contents

# Abbreviations

| | |
|---|---|
| BX | slip on the Passap |
| BY | background yarn |
| COL | carriage on left |
| COR | carriage on right |
| CY | contrast yarn or centre yarn in petal slip stitch |
| dec | decrease |
| EAN | every alternate needle |
| FNR | full needle rib |
| HP | holding position |
| KC | pattern knitting on the Brother |
| KCI | Brother electronic pattern knitting, with end needle selection |
| KCII | Brother electronic pattern knitting without end needle selection |
| MY | main yarn |
| N1C | needle 1 cam (Knitmaster) |
| NWP | non-working position |
| PC | point cam (Knitmaster electronic machines) |
| PP | punchcard pattern |
| PPE | punchcard pattern on elongation |
| PY | petal colour yarn |
| RC | row count |
| RH | right hand |
| st(s) | stitches |
| TD | tension dial |
| UWP | upper working position |
| WP | working position |
| WY | waste yarn |

# Introduction

Slip stitch is used to produce a surface texture on the purl side of the fabric in the same way as tuck stitch. For a long time it has been used mostly for this purpose with only an occasional exploration into its other uses. There are many similarities between tuck stitch and slip stitch: both cam settings use the non-selected needles as the patterning needles, both pattern on the purl side of the fabric and both rely on a strand of yarn across the non-selected needles on the purl side. When using either cam setting they both have restrictions as to the number of rows which can be knitted before a muddle occurs.

At first sight the differences between slip stitch and tuck stitch are hard to separate. Why then has tuck stitch been researched and developed whilst slip stitch has been neglected? The main difference between them is that in tuck stitch the strand of yarn which passes the non-selected needle is taken into the needle head without knitting and held there for several rows. In slip stitch the strand of yarn passes in front of the non-selected needles across the fabric, forming a float (*Fig. 1*). The significance of this difference has not been fully realized until now.

The loops which form in the needle head of a tuck stitch are the reason for the development of tuck stitch and the neglect of slip stitch. The tuck loops distort the fabric by pushing the stitches out of line, thus widening the knitting and forming interesting, patterned textures on either side of the fabric. Slip stitch seems to be capable only of producing surface textures on the purl side of the knitting. The texturing produced by slip stitch is rather flat and uninteresting when compared with tuck stitch. The strands of yarn across the surface of the knitting pull in the work, narrowing the width of the fabric.

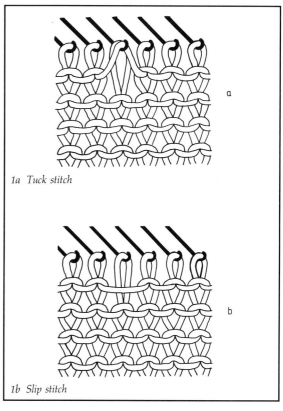

*1a Tuck stitch*

*1b Slip stitch*

The tuck stitch characteristic of collecting loops in the needle head means that tuck stitch has an inbuilt restriction in that the Japanese machines are capable of knitting no more than 6–8 loops of yarn before causing a muddle. Even the Passap with its capacity of perhaps 20 loops has a limit. The slip stitch characteristic of taking a strand of yarn across the front of the fabric is far more flexible, as will be shown as we explore and develop 'slip stitch', the neglected stitch.

# 1 Guidance and information

## THE SLIP SETTING

The slip setting has a different name on each make of machine:

1 Knitmaster – slip

2 Brother – part

3 Toyota – empty

4 Passap – BX

The Passap has other slip settings available such as GX and HX. GX is used for a free move across the needlebed whether the pushers are in work or not. The BX setting is the one mostly used in conjunction with the arrow keys to produce the intricate patterns on which we shall be working and – unless stated otherwise – is the setting to use when slip is specified.

For the sake of simplicity, 'slip' will be used throughout the book unless a particular machine is specified.

Note: Throughout this book any reference to a Passap knitting machine also refers to the Pfaff Duomatic machine.

## YARN GUIDE

The yarn that was used to knit the samples illustrated here is not of any particular brand. Most manufactur-ers tend to change their range of yarns and colours every year or two. I do not want there to be the restriction of trying to reproduce an exact copy of the samples. What I want to do is to encourage you to experiment and mix your own yarn.

There are more outlets than ever before which sell the most interesting fancy yarns. Try to buy as many fine yarns as you can afford so that they can be mixed and matched. By fine yarn I mean the industrial counts such as 2/30s, 2/24s, 2/20s and 2/16s which are usually marked inside the cone. Not all the labels inside the cones can be relied on as they are used to rewind small amounts from larger cones but if the yarn is a repeatable one then the label should be correct. Remember it is not only the chunky machines which will take more than one strand of yarn. If you can move away from the standard 4-ply yarn when you have mastered your machine, a whole new world will be opened up. The restriction placed on you by someone else deciding which colours should be used is lifted, giving a freedom of choice not usually available.

There are five branded yarns with a wide colour range which I keep in stock. They are Hobby, Astrakan, Silky, a 4-ply acrylic from Texere Yarns in Bradford which is similar to Artistic, and Forsells 2-ply wool. All of these yarns are well established, they are tried and tested for colour fastness and reliability and are easily obtainable (*see Yarn suppliers, page 155*). They mix very well with each other and with natural fibres to produce unique fabrics with unusual finishes.

# TENSION GUIDE

Tension is the most important feature of machine knitting. The way the machine stretches and distorts the fabric whilst it is being knitted makes it imperative that tension pieces are correctly dealt with and measured.

Wash and press every tension piece before attempting to knit a garment. When mixing different types of yarn it is important to find out how any particular yarn combination will react when washed. It is no good trying to sell a designer garment and then finding out that the fabric has stretched or shrunk after washing! Wash garments with a natural fibre content before despatch. Make sure that your customers know this and give them full details of how they can get the same result. This can save a lot of problems later on. Washing a tension piece also ensures that any distortion to the pattern shows up before the garment is knitted.

Each machine produces its own unique tension and it is often impossible to match exactly a tension produced by a designer. As the book has progressed I have worked on various makes and models of machines which has made me realize just how much the tension differs. Any reference to a specific tension is to be used only as a guide. The types of fabric I am aiming for are those with a soft fluid feel. Even jacquard fabrics can have this finish if a fine yarn and the correct tension is used. There is no need for 'cardboard' knitting once you have mastered the correct combination of yarn and tension.

There are numerous ways of checking and measuring a tension piece.

## Standard-gauge machines:
### normal tension piece

1  Cast on over 30/30 sts each side of 0. Knit 20 rows in the yarn, stitch and tension that you would like to use for the garment. Check that the fabric has the right feel to it. If not, alter the tension dial one whole number, smaller to tighten and firm up the fabric, larger to loosen

*2  Charting rulers*

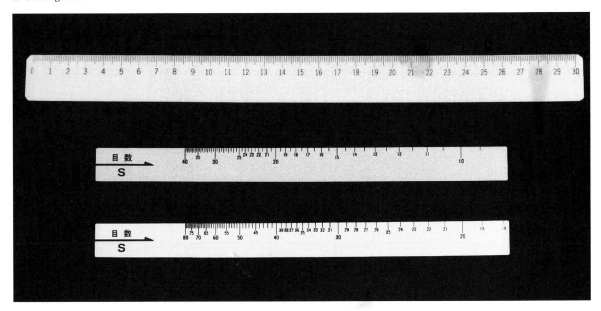

and soften it. Keep on altering the tension gradually, one dot at a time, until the fabric has the right weight and feel to it.

2 Knit 2 rows in CY yarn keeping the pattern correct. RC000.

3 Knit 30 rows in MY. Mark the 21st stitch each side of 0. Knit to RC60.

4 Knit 2 rows in CY.

5 Knit a further 20 rows in pattern and MY.

6 Cast off.

Mark the sample with the stitch size either by swiss darning or with a tie-on tag.

Pull the tension piece lengthways after allowing it to rest for a while, then steam press. If the work has been knitted on the ribber it should be left to relax overnight before it is steamed.

Wash the tension piece in fairly hot water to release any dressing in the yarn. Rinse well and allow to dry.

Steam press, allow to relax for a few minutes. The sample can now be measured in the usual way using either the green ruler or the ruler which belongs to your particular charting device (*Fig. 2*). If you do not own a charting device then buy a green ruler to simplify the calculations needed to produce a garment of the correct size.

## Chunky machines

Work the tension piece as above but halve the number of stitches and rows. To measure use the blue ruler which is specially designed for use with chunky machines or the measure that comes with your machine (*Fig. 2*).

## Motif blocks

Some of the samples are in obvious single-motif blocks. In this case I have measured the width and the depth of the motif and adapted the design to accommodate full or half motifs to simplify making up. The shaping of a garment can be worked between motifs, completely disguising where they occur.

## Sideways-knitted skirts

Tension samples for sideways-knitted skirts need a different approach from ordinary tension pieces.

Follow the instructions for knitting the panels. Knit at least two panels, following the details in the instructions (*see Knitting chart, Fig. 89*)

Change to waste yarn, knit at least 20 rows and strip off the machine. Give the panel a really good steam press. Wash the panel, spin in the washer, pull lengthways and hang to dry using a bar skirt hanger. These hangers grip the top of the panel, keeping it level at the top (*Fig. 3*). The fact that the panel is left to hang until it is dry allows it to stretch to its full length. There should be no need to press the skirt again. Whatever you do to it afterwards, the length will not alter as the shape and length have been set by allowing the skirt to hang whilst wet.

3 *Skirt panel in bar hanger*

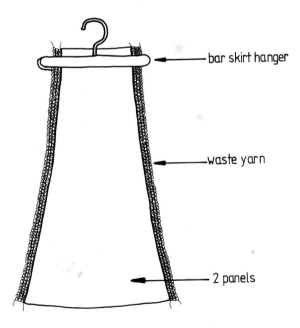

bar skirt hanger

waste yarn

2 panels

# PUNCHCARD INFORMATION

## Marking

1 To save space most punchcard patterns are marked in diagram form over 24 stitches but with only one repeat of the rows.

2 Different widths are marked with the appropriate stitch width.

3 Each pattern is marked for use on the standard punchcard machines. The pattern will have to be repeated until at least 36 rows have been marked. This is to ensure that the card will rotate when joined.

4 For electronic machines only one pattern width and depth need be marked.

5 The Passap Deco requires that the cards are marked for at least 30 rows, in reverse. The slip stitches are marked; the knit sections are left blank.

6 Most of the designs have been marked out with single marking to save space. In some cases the pattern can be elongated. This will be indicated, where it applies, by an E after the pattern number. These are the designs which can be knitted on the Passap. Any design with single marking not requiring elongation cannot be knitted on a Passap using the Deco as the Deco repeats every row.

7 If your machine does not have an elongation button then all designs will have to be double marked.

8 With a full-width design the pattern is marked on the card as shown. Some of the braids and edgings are

*4 How the pattern panel and needlebed relate*

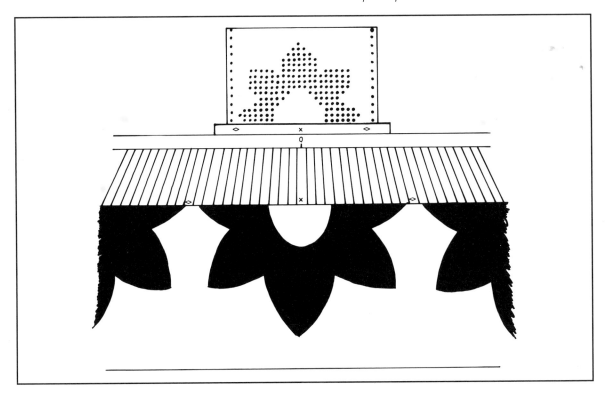

only 12 stitches wide and can be marked side by side on the same punchcard if you wish.

So that you will know which needles to select for the braids and edgings it is useful to understand how the punchcard, the pattern panel and the needlebed relate to each other. There are details in the manual for each make of machine. The pattern panel, where the punchcard is inserted, has markings which are repeated on the number strip of the needlebed (*Fig. 4*). Therefore any section of a punchcard can be selected to knit a braid on the relevant part of the needlebed.

# OPTIONAL ACCESSORIES

## Colour changers

A lot of the designs are produced by using frequent colour changes together with elongation. A colour changer is not essential but it helps to speed up the work. When we are using elongation as well as the colour changer, difficulty can be experienced in synchronizing the colour changes with the alteration to the needle selection. The problem can be overcome by punching both rows on the punchcard. Knitmaster 500 and 560 owners have to mark their mylar sheets in this way as the card changes on the right, making it impossible to use elongation and the colour changer. Select the appropriate method for your machine and use it throughout the following experiments.

### All Knitmaster punchcard machines, 370 and 270

1 Insert card and lock on row 1. Knit a few rows in WY. COR, knit to the left.

2 Change to MY and set carriage to slip. Knit to the right with card still locked.

3 Release card and set the L knob. Knit to the left.

### Brother punchcard machines

1 Insert card. Knit a few rows in WY. Change to MY and knit 2 rows. COR.

2 Set carriage to KC. Knit from right to left. The needles are now selected for the pattern.

3 Change yarn if necessary and move carriage to right to lock onto belt. Release card and set to elongation. Both part buttons in. Knit 2 rows. Continue with colour-change sequence.

### Brother 910 and 950

1 Knit a few rows in WY. Change to MY for 2 rows.

2 Move carriage to right outside the orange mark. Set carriage to KCII. Press CF. Button 4 up. Knit to left. Pattern needles selected.

3 Push in both part buttons. Continue to knit the colour sequence as instructed.

### Passap

The Passap colour changer works from the right-hand side of the machine and the Deco has elongation built into the patterning system. Full instructions are given in the Deco manual.

## Ribbers

A ribber is not essential as only two chapters in this book are devoted entirely to ribber work.

## Ribber transfer carriages

This accessory speeds up one of the most tedious jobs in ribber work, that of transferring the stitches from the front to the back bed.

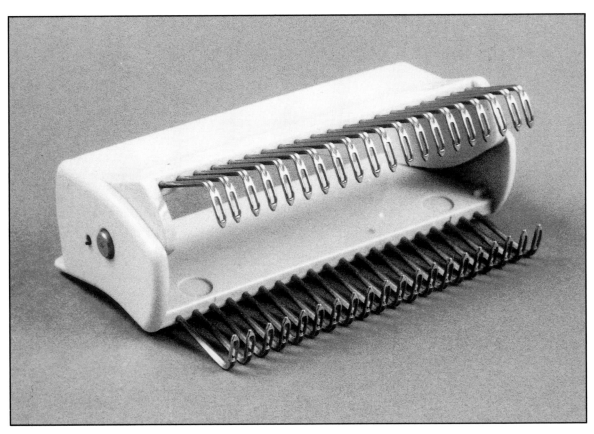

5 *Shadow lace transfer tool*

## Shadow lace transfer tool

Jaws (*Fig. 5*), as the shadow lace transfer tool is often called, is one of the most useful accessories there is and yet it is not very well known. It is the only tool which will transfer any number or combination of stitches up to 20 from the main bed to the ribber bed and back again if needed.

# 2 Basic slip stitch

Before we begin to explore slip stitch patterning it may help if there is some understanding of how the cam setting works. The simplified diagram of the underside of the 950 carriage in Fig. 6a shows the line the needles will follow when the carriage is set to normal. The cam buttons on a carriage operate levers on the underside of the carriage which alters the channel through which the needle butts can pass. When the slip buttons are depressed (*Fig. 6b*) the needles follow channel B, preventing them from

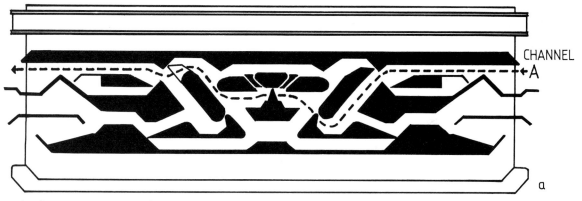

6a  Underside of carriage set to normal

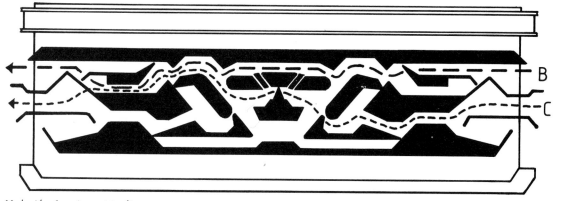

6b  Underside of carriage set to slip

moving forwards on the needlebed. Any needles in normal working position will not knit, giving a free move across the needlebed. This facility can be used in a number of ways.

## NON-SELECTIVE

1 To enable the carriage to pass from one side of the needlebed to the other without removing it from the needlebed.

2 In double-bed work, to hold stitches on one bed whilst the other bed knits, thus forming pintucks.

3 To allow the carriage free movement without knitting whilst stitches are held in B position. This is needed when the carriage is

>  a  at the wrong side for the yarn,
>
>  b  to be used to reset the punchcard after a mistake.

It is important to understand how the carriage can be moved from one side of the machine to the other without having to lift it off the needlebed. It is surprising how many people do this rather than set the machine to slip or hold depending on the position of the needles on the needlebed. If you are unable to gain enough confidence to understand how to make a free move across the needlebed then the machine is working *you*! This is not what knitting is about. To obtain the best from your machine it is essential that you gain full mastery over it. Rather than being afraid of the mechanics, try to find out how they work – after all, they are there to make life easier. Modern machines have been developed so that patterned knitting is almost as simple as plain knitting.

## SELECTIVE

Figure 6 (*bottom*) illustrates what happens to the needles when the slip cams are operated in conjunction with a punchcard. The non-selected needles, from the blank sections of the card, slot into channel B. The needles which are selected to knit, from the punched areas of the card, enter channel C. Both sets of needles enter separate channels and converge towards the end of the sequence where they are again separated into the appropriate channel by the punchcard. It is at this point that any change to the needle selection takes place.

The unpunched sections of the card stay in channel B but the needles connected to the punched sections of the card are pushed into channel C.

Selective slip stitch is the starting point of our exploration into this neglected setting.

There are two ways of selecting the needles.

### Hand selection

Hand selection is normally used to correct mistakes which have occurred when knitting.

When the machine is set to normal the slip setting allows the carriage a free move across the working position needles to knit those in holding position back to working position. The holding position needles are the ones which are hand selected.

To correct a row of stocking stitch, set the carriage to release. Place it at the same side as the row was begun. Unravel the knitting to the point where it went wrong. The stitches which were unravelled are placed in holding position. The machine is set to slip and the carriage is moved across the needlebed. The working position needles remain undisturbed and those in holding position knit back to working position to complete the row.

On the Passap, BX and pushers are used in the same way but with slightly different positions: the pushers of the needles which are to slip are placed in rest position and those which are to knit are placed in working position.

## Punchcard selection

The selection for pattern knitting is by punchcard or mylar sheet on the Japanese machines. Passap selection is by one of two methods: punchcard, or the pushers with the arrow keys.

It is not until we begin to delve into the mysteries of slip stitch that its full potential is realized. We use slip stitch or the slip setting many times without registering the fact. Using the holding position to

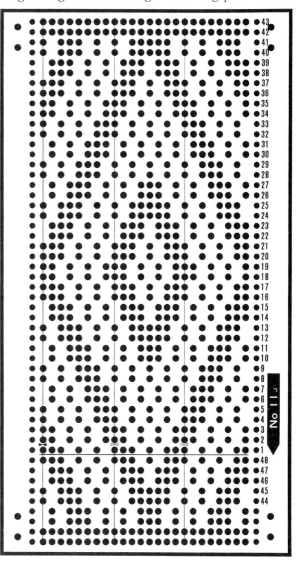

7 *Slip punchcards (courtesy Brother and Knitmaster)*

knit sideways-knitted skirts is an example of the wider use of slip stitch. Of course we are not using the slip cam setting, which this book is about to explore, but nevertheless it is a form of slip – as are Fair Isle, punch or thread lace and release stitch.

Each of the machines has a set of basic cards, some of which can be used for slip. To find out what sort of fabric the cards will produce and what appeals to you, it is a good idea to run through all those cards listed in the manual as suitable for slip.

A slip punchcard is easy to recognize (*Fig. 7*). Any card with large areas of punching and a small proportion of blanks can be used. As a general rule

the blank areas should be no wider than two or three stitches. The blank areas are the ones which slip and any float longer than three stitches will tend to catch and pull when the garment is worn.

Spotting a slip card for the Passap or an electronic machine is not so simple as they are usually marked in reverse. Cards with larger blank areas than those that are punched will produce the same effect as the conventional markings on the punchcard machines.

The patterns in the memory of the Brother 950 are marked the same as the conventional punchcards. This is presumably because it eliminates the need to operate the negative button which is used on the

8 *Ordinary slip stitch*

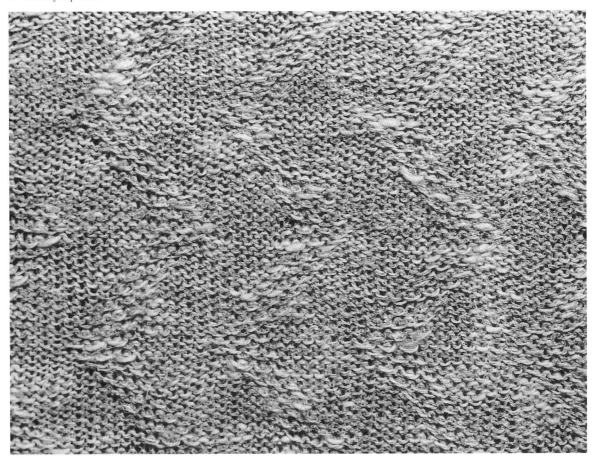

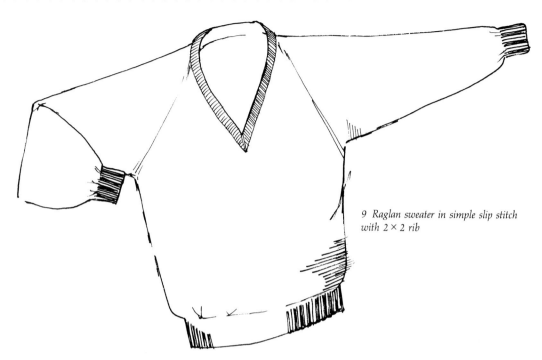

9 Raglan sweater in simple slip stitch
with 2 × 2 rib

other electronic machines. On an electronic machine there is a choice in the method of marking. The Passap has only one method which is extremely useful on slip and tuck as it saves hours of punching.

The standard slip punchcards with only one-stitch-wide slip sections do not produce very interesting surface patterns (*Fig. 8*). They can be used to good effect on menswear as the texture is not too obvious (*Fig. 9*).

To add weight to a fabric in a fine yarn, use card 1 rotating every row. The fabric produced by this method is very fine but it has more body than if the yarn were used to knit stocking stitch. On the knit side the fabric looks like stocking stitch. On the purl side there are short strands of yarn which look like weaving.

The pattern can be elongated by knitting each row twice. Even then the pattern is not very obvious; it is just twice as long. To obtain more pattern definition, select cards which have two adjacent stitches which slip. PP9E is such a design. It is marked for the Passap or the electronic machines. If it is to be used on a punchcard machine, punch it in reverse. If you own an electronic machine try using the widther button on

the conventional designs to double the pattern width (*Fig. 10a*). With this discovery slip stitch begins to take on a character of its own. If we combine the two stitch widths in the same design then the pattern becomes far more obvious and interesting (*Fig. 10b*). There are plenty of slip patterns available in the punchcard pattern books, many of them with a combination of stitch widths. Try them and see. We are not restricted to producing only solid fabrics with surface textures on the purl side when using slip cards. A few examples in the pattern books suggest leaving needles empty on certain parts of the needlebed. This technique is quite common in tuck stitch and is called tuck lace. The same technique when applied to slip stitch is not as well known.

There is an example of slip lace in *Stitch in Time* No. 42 which uses two needles in work, two needles out of work with eight knitted rows before the needle selection is altered.

Leaving one needle out of work and knitting two rows of slip tends not to be worth the effort of selecting the empty needles. There is no distortion of the fabric, simply strands of yarn passing over a gap in the knitting.

25

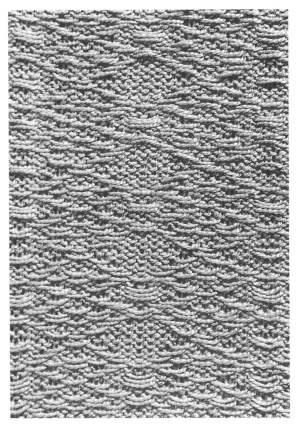

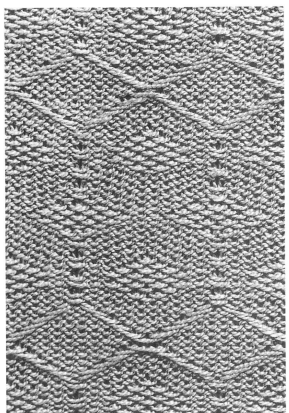

*10a  Two-stitch pattern*

*10b  Combination pattern*

We can make use of these strands of yarn which pass behind the knitting if we arrange them in an organized way. If a card is designed with the slip stitches one above another, the strands pull in the knitting forming the outer edge of a pleat (*PP10 on page 31*). Selected needles are left out of work to form the underfold of the pleat. The resulting fabric is most attractive (*Fig. 11*). The pleats are restricted to the punchcard width unless you own an electronic machine but it is one of the simplest and quickest ways of knitting pleats.

## KNITTING INSTRUCTIONS

1  Push to WP 97/97 needles each side of 0. The seam on each panel is then underneath the fold.

2  Leave needles 20, 44, 68 and 92 at the left of the needlebed in NWP and needles 5, 29, 53 and 76 at right of the needlebed in NWP.

3  Knit a few rows in WY so that weights can be attached before you begin to knit.

4  Use the crochet cast-on over the selected needles. Set the carriage to slip and knit the required number of rows. Knit as many panels as you need for your hip size.

The mylar sheet only needs one dot to be marked on each row. The negative button is used so that the pleat can then be adapted to any width.

11  *Slip pleats*

## VARIATION

PP3E will lend itself very well to this type of lace. Over the years there have been lots of needle set-ups used in combination with card 3 to produce a wide variety of designs. See the book *Card 3* by Kate Armitage. I suggest that you use elongation to obtain the eight rows of pattern used in the original slip lace.

In Fig. 12 (*left*), PP3E was used with a 2 × 2 needle arrangement. This needle selection means that one of the pattern sections of the card is not used. The machine is set to elongation. Knit eight rows in plain stocking stitch. The other eight rows of the pattern knit with one needle in two slipping. A ribber-type fabric with ridges at regular intervals is the result of

12  *One-colour and two-colour sample with 2 × 2 needle arrangement*

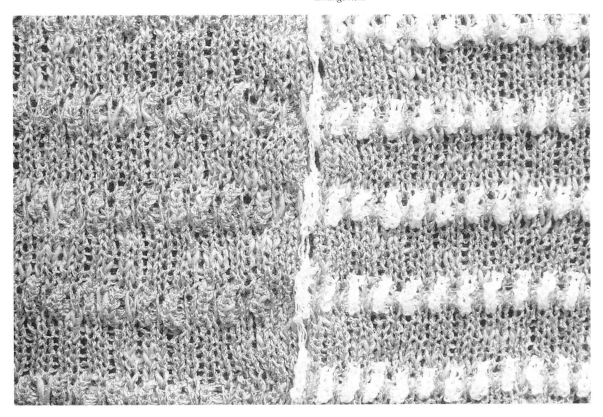

13 Tea-cosy pattern in single and two-colour ridges

this combination of card and needle setting. At last we are beginning to see the potential of the setting. The mixing of different-width slip sections, the knitting of up to eight rows before changing the needle selection and leaving needles out of work have suddenly shown what can be done with what appeared at first to be an insignificant setting.

As we have knitted eight rows before changing the needle selection without a muddle, it seems a good idea to experiment and see whether other textured effects can be produced. The mind immedi-

ately turns to the tea-cosy pattern. This stitch has been around for years, is simple to knit and very effective.

## Tea-cosy pattern

Select either PP1E or PP3E.

1 Cast on in WY the required number of stitches. Knit a few rows.

28

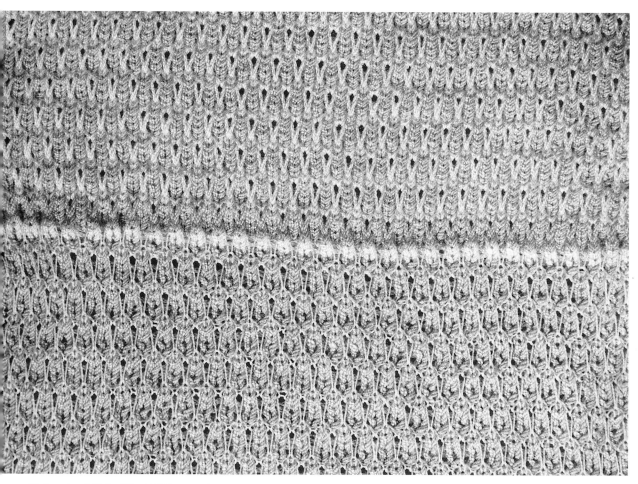

14 Samples of 8E in different thicknesses of yarn

2 Insert card, lock on row 1. Set machine to memorize pattern. Change to MY. *Knit 2 rows stocking stitch.

3 Set carriage to slip and knit at least 10 rows with the card locked.**
Repeat from * to ** for the desired length.

The result is a deeply ridged fabric which can be used to make a tea-cosy (Fig. 13). The number of rows knitted in slip stitch needs to be adjusted to the yarn thickness and to the effect you require.

Years ago I used this effect in a fine bouclé to form a frill for a bedspread. Twelve rows of slip were needed to produce a deep enough pleat. The strip was used sideways to give an illusion of pleated gathers and was most effective. I have forgotten how many thousands of rows had to be knitted but I am loath to redecorate the bedroom in any other colour in case another bedspread is needed!

Different textures and patterns can be produced by manipulating the cards in other ways. If the basic patterns which have two rows identical are set to elongation, and two rows of slip then two rows of stocking stitch are knitted, the pattern is interrupted and altered thus widening the scope of each card. For example, PP8E is card 2 with one row of punching between each needle change. The machine was set to elongate the pattern. The resulting fabric using a 4-ply yarn was rather bulky and produced a ridged effect on the purl side and texture on the knit side.

With colour introduced on the two stocking stitch rows the fabric is more interesting on the knit side. The contrast colour of the stocking stitch is held between the knit sections of the pattern rows and hauled up into the next two stocking stitch rows forming an outline to the raised sections which contain four rows of knitting.

To obtain more texturing on the knit side, a 4-ply yarn could be used for the pattern section and 2- or 3-ply yarn for the stocking stitch rows. The yarn can be either the same or a contrasting colour, depending on whether colour or texture is the most important feature of the fabric (*Fig. 14, top*). If a thin yarn is used in the stocking stitch then a different effect is produced (*Fig. 14, bottom*).

With the examples given above, select some of the basic cards and see what you can produce. The simple geometric cards have infinite possibilities and are far more likely to produce intriguing fabrics than the more intricate cards.

Should any of the designs appeal to you then it is a good idea to repunch the card with every two rows of pattern separated by two full rows of punching. In fact it is a good idea to work through the basic cards repunching them with two rows of holes between each pattern change. If the thought of all that marking and punching sounds too much like hard work, then teach the children whilst they are young! When I bought my first machine there were arguments over whose turn it was to punch. Now they are older and wiser and I have an electronic machine.

It is when we begin to manipulate the cards and play around with them that all the possibilities begin to be revealed. The introduction of colour changes when the pattern alters gives an indication that the knit side of the fabric can be just as interesting as the purl side.

The tea-cosy pattern could have pleats in alternating colours or the stocking stitch rows could be knitted in a contrasting colour. This adds interest on the purl side (*Fig. 13*).

In the variation described on page 27, colour can be introduced on the eight rows which have slip sections. The resulting fabric gives a clear indication that the use of a second colour on the slip sections can make the colour seem as if it has been slotted through the fabric rather than knitted in. The eight rows of colour stand off from the fabric in a far more obvious way than in the original (*Fig. 12, right*).

The slip lace mentioned earlier was used on the knit side. On the original garment the pattern shape was emphasized by a coloured border. The colour must be changed when the needle selection is altered. Failure to do so can totally alter the design, as will be shown throughout the following chapters.

*Punchcard pattern sheet 1*

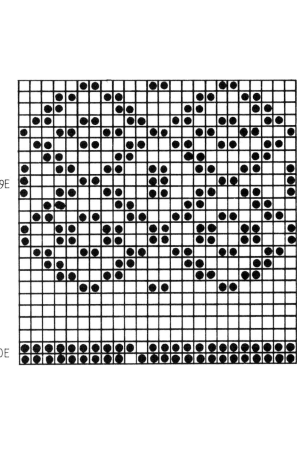

15 Autumn scene punchcard
Row 14 Change MY for water colour
  17 Change CY for leaves
  38 Change CY for hills
  41 Move CY into main feeder
   Insert new CY for heather
  53 Change CY for sky
  60 Move CY into main feeder
   Insert new CY for clouds
  88 Change CY to background colour

# 3 Multicoloured slip stitch

## FAIR ISLE

Fair Isle is perhaps the most popular setting on the machine. After stocking stitch has been mastered, Fair Isle is usually the first step towards patterned knitting. It is, I suspect, the reason some people buy a knitting machine in the first place. The prospect of being able to knit all those colourful designs, no matter how complicated, without reference to a chart inspires many a new machine knitter. Indeed it is not a difficult stitch to understand as it is visual. What you see on the punchcard is what appears on the knitting: a smooth, two-colour fabric with the colours appearing as if by magic where the punchcard determines they should.

Fair Isle is a form of slip stitch which allows two colours to be knitted in one row at the same time. The hand knitter follows a chart which shows when to change yarn to the second colour. The first colour is introduced once more and the second colour is stranded across the back of the fabric and so on to the end of the row.

On the machine the principle is the same but it is the punchcard which determines where the yarn changes occur. The punched holes knit the contrast yarn, i.e. the yarn in feeder 2. The unpunched holes knit the main yarn, i.e. the yarn in feeder 1. The yarn changes take place as the carriage is moved across the needlebed. At the same time the pattern for the next row is being selected by the pattern cams in readiness for the next movement of the carriage.

On a machine, Fair Isle knitting can be produced as quickly as stocking stitch. The origins of traditional Fair Isle designs are rather obscure. Whole books have been written on the subject of its design and history for both hand and machine knitters. However, my brief here is to cover the slip setting as it applies to the machine, and not to delve into the mysteries of this popular form of colour knitting.

There are a number of effects which can be achieved by varying either the yarn or the punchcard but using the same knitting method.

1 Traditional Fair Isle involves frequent colour changes to either the main or the contrast yarn to produce subtle shading through the design. The patterns are usually abstract designs or inanimate objects in border form (*see colour plate 1*). For more details and patterns see *The Complete Book of Traditional Fair Isle Knitting* by Sheila McGregor.

2 Modern Fair Isle designs are usually bold and knitted in strong contrasting colours. A recent development has been a collection of designs with pigs, frogs and teddy bears, etc. in various colour combinations. Geometric shapes lend themselves very well to this treatment and they are strongly in evidence.

3 Picture Fair Isle, another modern development, is very popular. It differs from the previous category in that the colours and designs are selected to produce realistic scenes. Ginny Hubble was one of the first designers to produce picture knitting using a punchcard, in the early 1970s. I designed the autumn scene

(*colour plate 2*) in 1979. It proved to be a bestseller. The illusion that there are more than two colours in a row is created by the way the yarn is changed. The punchcard in Fig. 15 details these changes. Only yarn with soft natural colours should be used to give a realistic appearance to the design.

4 Embossed Fair Isle is produced by using different textures of yarn which are usually in the same or a toning colour. The yarn with the rough texture rises above the smooth shiny one, giving an embossed effect to the fabric.

5 All-over Fair Isle is knitted using a punchcard where there is no apparent beginning or end to the pattern. The trick is to allow the design to overlap on each corner of the card to form a new shape where they meet (*Fig. 16*).

6 Self-colour Fair Isle is a technique which is used to produce a lightweight fabric with double thickness. Instead of using a double-knitting yarn which could strain the machine, it is a good idea to use two ends of the same colour 4-ply yarn on the Fair Isle setting. The fabric is much softer and lighter than one knitted in double knitting. An added bonus is that the purl side of the fabric looks as if it has been woven and can be used as a substitute for weaving if your machine does not have a weaving facility.

7 Punch lace uses the Fair Isle cams but unlike Fair Isle there are virtually no floats. The two yarns which are used are of different thickness. The fine yarn in feeder 2 knits the punched areas of the card. Blank areas of card knit both thicknesses together, eliminating the large floats which would form behind them.

## Passap single-bed Fair Isle

The Passap method of single-bed Fair Isle is totally different from the Japanese method. With the Passap system each colour has to be knitted individually. There are two ways of selecting needles:

1 Simple two-colour Fair Isle can be knitted using the BX setting, the pushers and the left arrow key.

2 The more complicated designs need to be selected by punchcard.

The knitting method is the same as for simple Fair Isle but the Deco does the selecting using the punchcard. The pushers are scooped up by the Deco and selected according to the pattern.

Each method entails knitting four rows to produce two actual rows of knitting.

## TWO COLOURS IN A ROW

We have discussed Fair Isle, which is two-colours-in-a-row slip, where the two colours are knitted-in on the same row. The next step is to knit the two colours individually, one colour at a time in two-row sequences. There is some mystique surrounding these patterns which do not bear any apparent relationship to the punchcard. The fabric produced by this method of knitting is like Fair Isle on the knit side but on the purl side there are virtually no floats. The punchcards are arranged in such a way that only one or two stitches are slipped at a time which gives the illusion, on the purl side, that there are no floats.

The punchcards used for knitting maze and mosaic patterns are not difficult to select. A card designed for slip usually has more punched holes than blank spaces. The unpunched sections are not usually more than two stitches wide. In most of the instruction manuals, at least one card is selected for the treatment. After selecting various cards using these principles it becomes obvious that maze and mosaic patterns are different (*Fig. 17*).

There are similarities:

1 Each requires single unpunched squares in two-row sequences which are broken by two rows of punching.

2 Each is knitted in two-row sequences.

*16 All-over Fair Isle* (opposite)

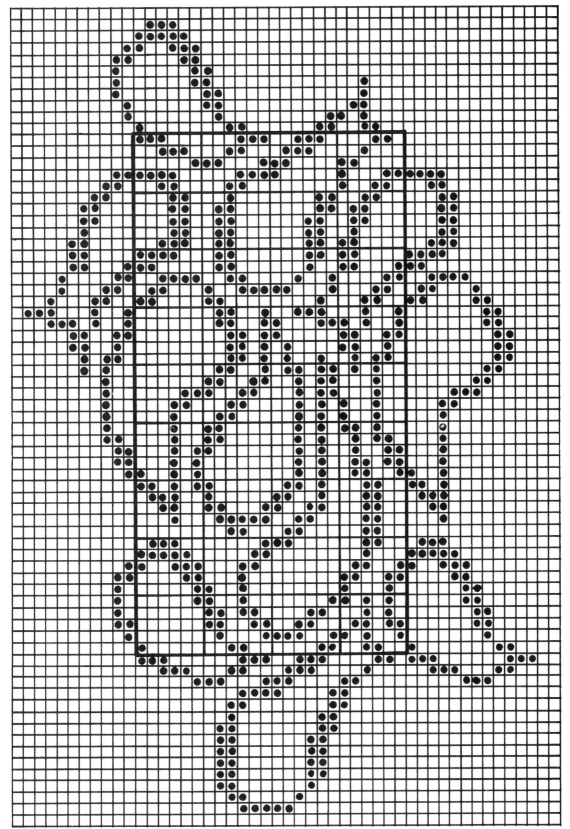

35

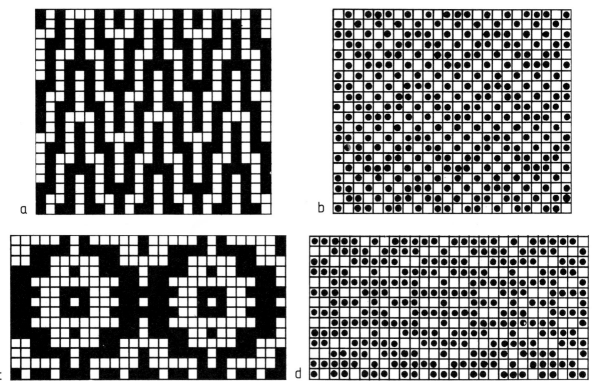

17a  Maze design chart
  b  Punchcard conversion chart
  c  Mosaic design chart
  d  Punchcard conversion chart

3 Each produces complex patterns which dazzle the eye and confuse the brain.

Where they differ is that a maze pattern produces just that — a maze-type pattern composed of various combinations of horizontal and vertical stripes in two colours which form geometric patterns on the knit side of the fabric. A mosaic pattern is less formal with fewer unbroken lines. The designs can be in recognizable shapes such as hearts and crosses which are formed by small groups of interlocking stitches.

These differences outline the way in which to select the correct punchcard for each pattern type. If we can learn to understand what each section of pattern will produce we should be well on the way to solving the mystery of these patterns.

## Maze patterns

A punchcard for maze knitting has only two parts. The cards are composed of different arrangements of these two sections:

1 The punched areas,́ when knitted in two-row colour sequences, always produce two-colour horizontal stripes.

2 Every alternate space is punched for two rows. On the following two-row sequence the in-between spaces are punched (*see PP2E*). When changing colour every two rows the card knits vertical stripes.

To check the above statement, use either card 1 on elongation, Knitmaster card 7, FK card 5, Brother card 2 (820, 830 and 840 only) or PP2E. When the sample is being knitted, two layers of fabric are formed. The

36

knit side is hidden from view by the slip bars when the work is on the machine and it is difficult for the mind to grasp just what is happening. A breakdown of the knitting method should help.

Although we are knitting in two-row colour sequences the pattern is four rows long.

Rows 1 and 2 of a sequence are always knitted in colour 1.

Rows 3 and 4 of a sequence are always knitted in colour 2.

It is this repetition which forms the vertical stripes.

## KNITTING INSTRUCTIONS

### Maze patterns

These punchcard designs require frequent colour changes. To synchronize the punchcard, the colour changer and the elongation button, different procedures are followed for each make of machine (*see Chapter 1, Colour changers*).

Begin the colour changes halfway through the sequence to set up the pattern correctly. Passap knitters will be quite familiar with this approach. If you begin to pattern at the beginning of the sequence there will not be the required colour for the slipped stitches on rows 1 and 2.

Knit two rows of colour 2 using the second row to select for the pattern.

1  Change to colour 1, knit 2 rows. RC2.
Row 1 knits the first stitch and slips the second to the end of the row.
Row 2 is identical to row 1.

2  Knit 2 rows in colour 2. RC4.
Row 3 slips the first stitch and knits the second stitch to the end of the row.
Row 4 is identical to row 3.

*Note* The stripes will only form if the colour is changed when the card selection alters.

If you have a machine which preselects the pattern you can check whether it is correct or not. The colour must always change when the needle selection changes. The yarn in the feeder should be the same colour as the stitches on the needles which have been selected.

To check whether you are correct on a machine which does not preselect the needles, move the card lock lever forwards and check that the levers which have been selected to the forward position are the ones which correspond to the stitches which hold the same colour yarn as that in the yarn feeder (*Fig. 4*).

Four movements of the carriage are required to produce two rows of knitting. Examine the punchcard again and you should be able to see the vertical lines more clearly. The only stitches which appear on the knit side are those which are punched. The blank sections on the card, which have slipped, disappear completely to form slip bars on the purl side of the fabric.

When this basic design is taken in isolation and placed in a punched area, in the shape of either diamonds, triangles, squares and zigzags, interesting maze patterns are formed. With these intricate designs it is hard to visualize just how the design will look when knitted.

### Translating a punchcard to a graph pattern

Whilst reference to maze and mosaic patterns for the machine have been around for a long time, no one has successfully explained, until recently, how to translate the punchcards onto graph paper to show how the pattern will turn out when it has been knitted. (See *Mosaic Floatless Fair Isle* by Kathleen Kinder and *A Machine Knitter's Guide to Creating Fabrics* by Susanna Lewis and Julia Weissman.)

Turn to the slip section of your instruction manual. Most types of machine have a sample of two-colour slip knitting which produces a maze pattern. Select the appropriate card. Cover the picture of the finished pattern and using the punchcard mark out the design onto graph paper in the following way, bearing in mind that the punchcard is punched for two rows of pattern but you *only mark one row on the graph paper*.

1  Odd-numbered rows on the graph paper: mark the punched areas.

2 Even-numbered rows on the graph paper: mark only the blank squares.

The final pattern is revealed as you work through the punchcard. Check with the manual illustration to see that you have succeeded. My feelings, when I had checked a punchcard using this method and found it was so easy, are hard to describe. That the solution should be so simple is incredible. We now have at our disposal a vast array of designs which will enable us to knit two-colour fabrics virtually without floats.

Acknowledgement is due to Kathleen Kinder for her help in solving the secrets of these designs. We were both working on the problem of translating them to graph paper. Kathleen found the missing link in Barbara Walker's book *Charted Knitting Designs,* a book which is not readily available in this country. This discovery means that it is possible to have any design you wish within certain limits. Slightly different rules apply when designing either maze or mosaic patterns but the same principles apply when translating the design to a punchcard. We shall continue working with maze patterns to explain exactly how the translation of the designs is done.

## Designing maze patterns

*Rules*

1 No more than one stitch to slip at a time.

2 Each single line on the graph paper represents two rows of knitting.

3 Odd-numbered rows can have any number of squares marked but only single blanks.

4 Even-numbered rows must have single squares marked.

5 Vertical lines must begin and end on an odd-numbered row.

6 Vertical lines must always be an odd number of rows.

7 The finished design must be an even number of rows so that when the pattern is repeated the colour sequence remains constant.

Study the punchcard pattern books to see what sort of design you should be drawing. Stick to geometrics for the moment so that you are in no danger of straying into the area of mosaic patterns. Remember that the finished pattern must consist of horizontal and vertical stripes which meet at right angles to form geometric shapes. These angles are distorted when the fabric is knitted because the horizontal striped sections have twice as many rows as the vertical stripe sections.

To help with the drawing of the design, mark the graph paper every odd (alternate) row with the appropriate row number and make sure that you keep within the rules. The most important ones are rules 3 and 4.

After you have designed a pattern the next step is to translate the design from graph paper to a punchcard. The method is quite simple. If the rows on the graph paper are numbered as in the diagram in Fig. 18 you should not lose your place.

**To convert a graphed design to a punchcard**

1 On odd-numbered rows, fill in all the marked sections from the graph leaving the unmarked sections blank.

2 On even-numbered rows, fill in the squares which are blank on the graph leaving the marked squares blank.

Work through the design until you have completed the conversion to the punchcard. It is a good idea to mark out the conversion onto graph paper first, using single markings so that any faults which show up can be corrected quite easily.

To test your design, transfer it to a punchcard either as it is with the machine set to elongation or redraw the punchcard repeating each row twice. I chose to use the elongation button as it saves a lot of punching but if you have a punchcard machine and the pattern is less than 30 rows long you will have to punch the pattern twice anyway in order to allow the card to rotate.

The pattern in Fig. 18 was drawn as an experiment to test the theory. It worked beautifully except for

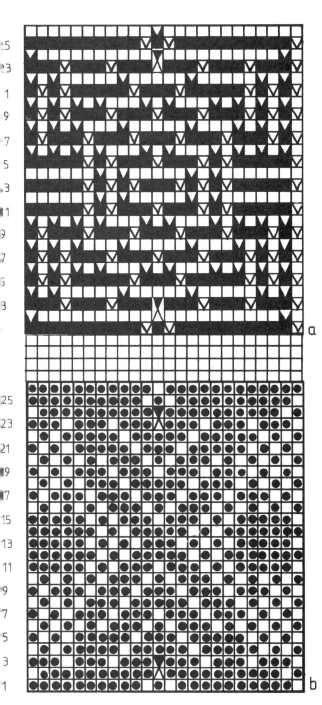

slip stitches, odd rows

colour 2

slip stitches, even rows

design fault

colour 1

18a Maze design chart with symbols
 b Punchcard conversion chart

one section which, despite following the rules I have laid out, left the punchcard pattern with two blanks one above the other. If this happens there is a fault in your pattern. To overcome this it is necessary to check the design as it is being planned.

The international symbol for slip is a 'V' mark. As you draw the design, mark each slip stitch with a V in a contrast colour (*Fig. 18a*). On odd-numbered rows of graph paper the V will be on the blank squares. On even-numbered rows of graph paper the V will be on the marked squares. Each V mark should be isolated. *If these symbols form a vertical line the pattern is wrong.* The V marks on the graph are the blanks on the punchcard. To simplify the card marking, Kathleen Kinder in her mosaic book suggests that the blanks are outlined on the card. Leave these squares unpunched and punch out the blank ones.

To check your design, knit at least two full patterns, changing colour every two rows as instructed for maze knitting. If you do this you will see how your design joins up. When I knitted the pattern in Fig. 18 there was a fault at the point where the slip stitches were two deep. The punchcard was altered so that the slip stitches were separated by a punched square which corrected the fault (*Fig. 26*).

Maze patterns are easy to design. The punchcards are also fairly easy to identify even when there is no photograph or knitted sample with the punchcard. Just look for punchcards which have only two sorts of marking:

1 Completely punched sections.
2 Sections with every alternate needle punched for two rows.

The two sections can be arranged in any way. They are usually geometrically shaped. To check a ready-punched card you should now be able to mark out, on graph paper, the finished maze following the rules given at the beginning of the section.

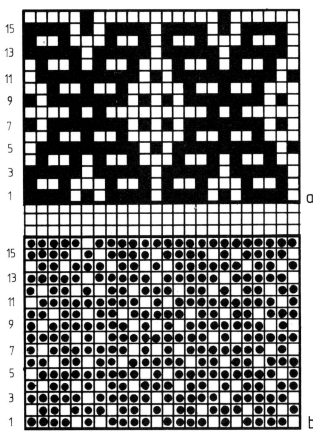

*19a Mosaic design chart*
*b Punchcard conversion chart*

## Mosaic patterns

Mosaic patterns are knitted in exactly the same way as maze patterns, i.e. in two-row colour sequences. The stripe sequence is not as obvious because the vertical and horizontal stripes are broken and the design looks more like Fair Isle (*Fig. 19*).

Despite the geometric appearance of a mosaic pattern the punchcards look more muddled than those for the maze (*Fig. 17b and 17d*). The principles of design are similar to the maze but because the patterns are more complex there is a greater risk that your design will have built-in faults. We have

established that a slip stitch is usually just a single blank or mark but because this is mosaic knitting as opposed to maze knitting, two consecutive stitches can be slipped. Remember that slip stitches should be in isolation surrounded by stitches which are to knit.

When designing mosaics, keep to the geometric tile patterns at first. This way your understanding of mosaics will be consolidated and it should be possible to develop your knowledge to design less regular, more natural shapes. To simplify the mosaic designing I took a rectangular block which I knew followed the rules for mosaic patterns and built up the design from these blocks which can be of any size (*Fig. 20*). It was then possible to see that certain sections could be removed from the design to give it a more flowing appearance. The design in Fig. 19 was based on such a block.

*20 Mosaic block*

Mosaic patterns, being less regular than maze patterns, sometimes need to have the gaps in a design filled in to ensure that there are no long floats. It is here that the two different elements are likely to overlap. The combination of maze and mosaic knitting produces interesting patterns with a variety of shapes, lines and dots which successfully hide the fact that the pattern has been knitted in two-row sequences of colour (*Fig. 21*).

The fabric produced by maze and mosaic knitting is like stocking stitch in two colours. Most of the fabric is single thickness with only the occasional overlap of the two yarns where the slip-stitch bars pass behind the held stitches. It is the ability of the slipped stitches to hide the second colour which makes slip stitch such an interesting subject to investigate. The knit side of the fabric looks like Fair Isle but the lack of floats on the back intrigues anyone who reverses the fabric (*Fig. 22*). The colours seem to pop in and out of the knitting at will but now the mystery has been solved we can understand what is happening.

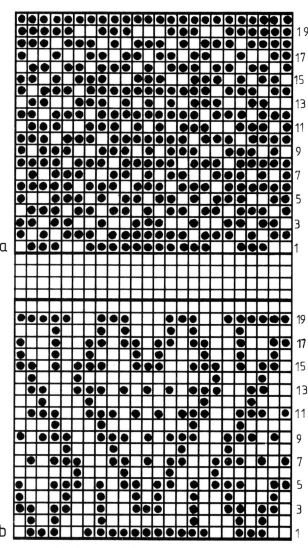

*21a Punchcard conversion chart*
  *b Design chart for combination pattern*

# Maze and mosaic knitting on the Passap

The Passap Deco pattern system requires only the patterning needles to be marked. This is the opposite of the Japanese way. Consequently the card marking

is much simpler as only the slip stitches are marked and there is a lot less punching to do.

It is harder to visualize the pattern which will be produced from a punchcard marked in this way but as long as you remember that the blanks represent the knitted sections and the marked squares are the slip stitches, you should not have too much difficulty converting the punchcard to a graph pattern of the design.

Use prepunched card number 39 (*Fig. 23*). The graph is marked on one row for each row marked on the punchcard. (All the Deco cards have single marking because the Deco knits each row twice or four times depending on which setting you select.)

1 On odd-numbered rows all the blanks on the punchcard are marked on the graph paper. The marked squares are left blank.

2 On even-numbered rows the marked squares are marked and the blanks are left blank.

The pattern which this card will knit is slowly revealed as you mark the graph.

To design a pattern for the Passap, follow the rules and instructions for the Japanese machines making sure that the design fits into 40 stitches. Use the V marking to check your design. When converting your design from a graph to a punchcard the V marks form the punchcard markings. Simply copy them from the graph on to the punchcard until it is complete.

To knit the design use BX with the left arrow key and knit in two-row sequences in two colours.

## VARIATIONS

The two-row, two-colour sequence can be altered by introducing more colours. It is better to have an odd number of colours as this breaks up the design. If three colours are used the first colour will not appear on the first row of pattern until the third repeat, giving a new look to the design. Maze patterns lend themselves more easily to this treatment than do mosaics (*Fig. 24*). Mosaic patterns tend to have definite shapes which enclose the second colour. The

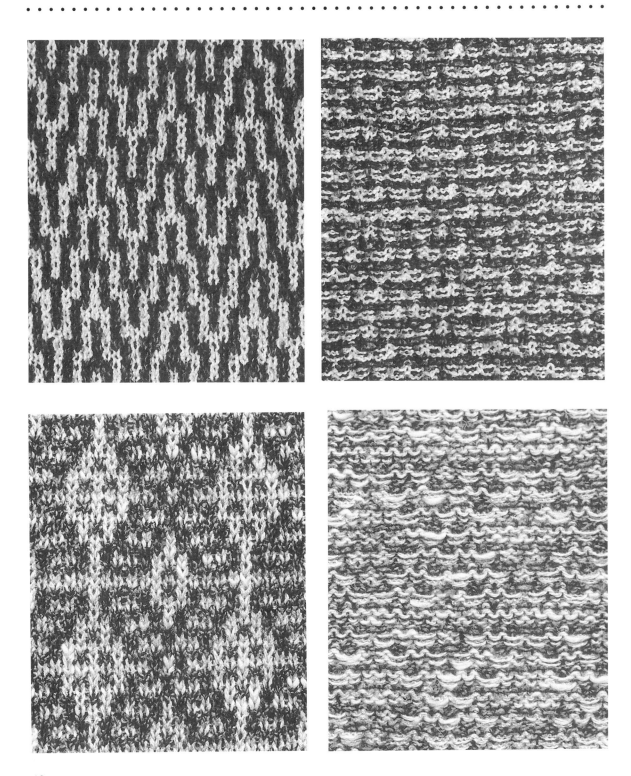

22 Maze knitting: knit side (top left) *and reverse side* (top right);
mosaic knitting: knit side (bottom left) *and reverse side* (bottom
right)

23 Passap card 39 (courtesy Passap)

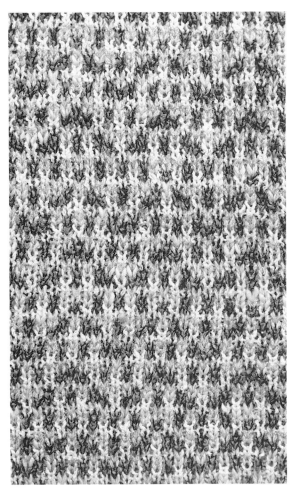 

*24 Three-colour maze (left) and three-colour mosaic (right)*

introduction of a third colour seems to break up the shapes. Extra colours can be introduced when a new sequence is begun ( *Fig. 24, right*).

As I become more familiar with the mosaic patterns their potential increases. The two-colour fabric of virtually single thickness with a minimum of floats is ideal for children's wear. Floaty fabrics which will drape are possible. For evening wear a combination of plain yarn and one with a lurex thread would be stunning.

## Slip lace

The lace mentioned in Chapter 2 and called slip lace was created by leaving needles out of work and slipping lots of rows to form interesting surface textures on the knit side. The fabric, although called slip lace, was rather bulky with lots of untidy floats. If different thicknesses of yarn are used when knitting maze and mosaic patterns then a more recognizable form of lace can be produced without a lace carriage (*Fig. 25*).

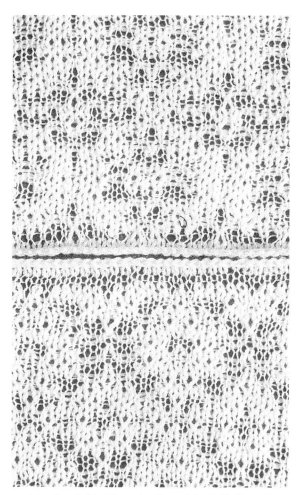

25 Maze lace (left) and samples of mosaic lace with the same pattern card, yarns reversed (right)

Although there are no actual empty needles the fabric looks like punch lace. If different colours are used as well as different thicknesses of yarn, then a float-free, lightweight fabric results which has two colours that are completely separate, not mixed together as in punch lace. Mosaic patterns seem to have more impact than maze designs as the colours tend to be in blocks rather than stripes. However, if a maze design has a number of punched areas, the resulting horizontal stripes, in different thicknesses of yarn, are most attractive. Figure 26 shows the corrected punchcard for Fig. 18.

The greater the difference between the yarn thicknesses the more interesting and open is the lace effect as the tension is set to accommodate the thick yarn and remains the same throughout the knitting. Try using different textures as well as different thicknesses to produce unusual fabrics. Most knitting machines have a slip setting and this way of using maze and mosaic patterns will enable those without any of the lace facilities to produce this simple form of lace.

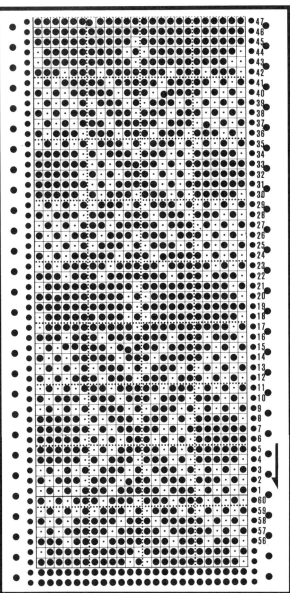

26 Corrected maze punchcard

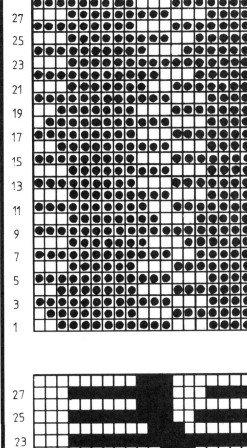

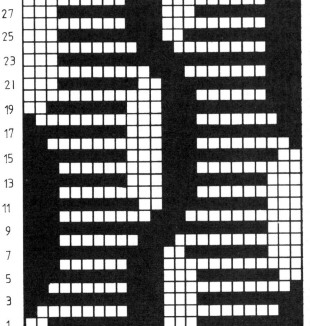

27a Design chart for block slip   b Punchcard conversion chart

## Two-colour block stitch

There is another type of punchcard which is knitted in two-row, two-colour sequences. It was this kind of design in *Modern Machine Knitting* which gave me the clue to solving the mosaic mystery. They differ from the previous two pattern types in two ways.

*28a Design for three colours in a row*
  *b Conversion to a punchcard*

1 The slip stitch sections can be three or four stitches wide.

2 There is no attempt to disguise the two-row, two-colour sequence of the pattern. Indeed, the stripe effect is a most important part of the design.

The larger groups of slipped stitches form solid blocks of either colour 1 or colour 2, depending on which row the block is begun. The shape and colour of the blocks are altered by the way the slip blocks are arranged on the punchcard. We are still in two-row sequences with the stitches being slipped for no more than two rows. The punchcards are quite distinctive (*Fig. 27*). Large sections are punched with blocks of up to four unpunched squares arranged in a pattern over the card with two rows of punching separating each block of blanks.

The fabric is similar in weight and feel to maze and mosaic knitting. There are a number of floats but not enough to cause too many problems when used for a garment. There is a slight distortion of the stripes as they are gathered into the slip sections where they occur. This is the attraction of the fabric. Unlike some of the maze designs, the two-colour stripes, interrupted at intervals by solid blocks of colour, are pleasing to the eye. I have called these designs 'block slip' to distinguish them from ordinary slip stitch.

### Designing block slip cards

1 Colour in all the odd-numbered rows.

2 Rub out the shape you would like to knit (this shape will be in colour 2).

3 On the blank rows fill in the shape you would like to knit in colour 1.

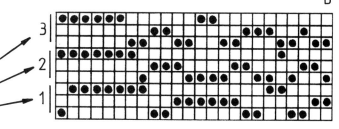

# THREE COLOURS IN A ROW

Fair Isle is a method of slip knitting which allows two colours to be knitted in one row at the same time. Maze and mosaic knitting illustrate the use of two colours in a row, each knitted separately, to produce an almost float-free fabric. To enable us to have more than two colours in one row the punchcards have to be altered to allow for the extra colours to be knitted. The slip setting must be used which means knitting one colour in a row at a time. Each colour requires a line of the punchcard to itself. When the design is knitted the resulting pattern is an intriguing Fair Isle effect with, say, three colours in a row. We are not restricted to three colours but as the floats are increased each time another colour is added, the fabric becomes more bulky and difficult to handle.

*30 Tam-o'-shanter, scarf and gloves in stocking stitch and Fair Isle*

*29 Slipover*

## Punchcard adaptation

Any design with an outline can be split into three colours. Each colour is given a line to itself. It is easier to draw the design onto graph paper as it appears for Fair Isle. The paisley design used to illustrate all-over Fair Isle in Fig. 16 is ideal for the treatment. The centre of each shape is lightly filled in with pencil to give the three colours you are to use (*Fig. 28a*).

48

The card has been designed to ensure that there are three colours in every row. This simplifies the knitting as a regular sequence is easy to remember. The graph paper and punchcard are marked off at three-row intervals and numbered so that it is quite clear which row has been reached (*Fig. 28b*). It is then a simple matter to mark out each colour on the appropriate row. This method of marking also means that you can check that every square on each three-row section is marked. If any are blank your design will be incorrect. Unlike Fair Isle, every stitch must be punched at some time in each three-row sequence.

The paisley design is 45 rows long which makes it tedious to convert to three colours in a row. Select a pattern with similar properties and no more than 25 rows long, from one of the punchcard books or use the design in Fig. 105 (*Chapter 10*).

We are still working in two-row colour sequences. Each colour is knitted separately for two rows. Because of the frequent changes of colour it is easier to use a colour changer. If your machine does not have an elongation facility or you have a Knitmaster 500 or 560 machine, then every row will have to be double marked. A 25-row pattern adapted to three colours in a row becomes 75 rows with single marking. Double marking increases this to 150 rows which is the length of a mylar sheet.

When the principle is understood, turn to the punchcard pattern books which have sections devoted to multicoloured single-bed slip. Not many of the patterns have three colours in every row. Most tend to have sections with only two colours at intervals throughout the pattern. As long as you mark the card or mylar sheet with care, these designs are quite simple to knit (*Figs. 29 and 30; see Chapter 10 for pattern.*)

*Punchcard pattern sheet 2*

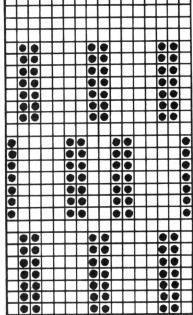

12E

Small flower 16sts wide

11E

Poppy 20sts x 32 rows

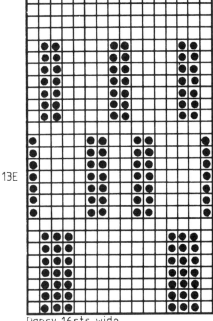

13E

Pansy 16sts wide

# 4 Petal slip stitch

As discussed in Chapter 1, the normal use of the slip setting is to enable us to pass the yarn across the front of the non-selected needles, on the purl side, to produce surface patterns. If we decide to use the knit side as the right side, the yarn is still across the non-selected needle on the purl side but it is not seen.

When the yarn colour is changed every two rows, the colours are introduced along the row, seemingly without floats, to produce maze patterns. What happens if this technique is taken further? Various samples using selective slip stitch with a colour change have produced some interesting stitch samples, but it is to the Passap we turn for the more spectacular effects.

The Passap is a machine with the capability of holding stitches for more rows than any other knitting machine, before causing a muddle. In *Passap Model Book 41* the cover design used slip stitch for 16 rows before changing the needle selection. Until now it has been believed that Japanese machines were not capable of producing this type of single-bed fabric. However, after various experiments it has now proved to be within the reach of us all. Using the Brother 910 to test the theory I discovered that it is possible.

With a pattern base of ten stitches the next step was to test the method on the Knitmaster 370 Fine Knitter, the 30-stitch pattern repeat being a straightforward translation (*Fig. 31*). I expected a different result on the Knitmaster system because, unlike the J-B and Toyota systems, all the needles stay in normal

*31 Fine-knit punchcard (Passap adaptation)*

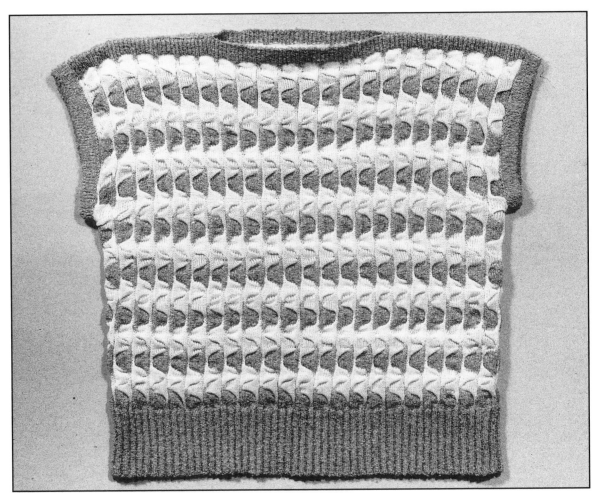

*32 Fine-knit slipover*

working position until the carriage is moved across the needlebed, selecting as it knits. No problems were encountered and the experiment was a success, thus proving that all Japanese patterning systems can knit many more rows without muddles than was first thought. What surprised me most of all was the quality of the fabric and the fact that it was virtually indistinguishable from that of the Passap. At last those who have longed for 'Passap' effects can produce heavily textured fabrics on their present machines.

The unusual shapes are made when the colour is changed at the same time as the needle selection. The pull of the slipped stitches when the needle selection changes, distorts and ruches the knitting, forcing it into surprising shapes. Who would have thought that groups of ten stitches, two being slipped for sixteen rows whilst the remaining ones are knitted, would produce a D-shaped quilted-look bubble in the fabric (*Fig. 32*)? The Passap version had four colours in the pattern but by using only three colours the pattern was altered. The D shapes in each colour changed

52

direction on their respective alternate pattern blocks, thus giving another dimension to the fabric.

The petal slip stitch came about quite by accident. Once it became apparent that the Japanese machines were capable of taking as many as 16 rows without a muddle, the search for more punchcards became a challenge. Nowhere in the Japanese punchcard pattern books could I find this approach to slip stitch.

There was a clue in the *Australian Machine Knitters Magazine*, April 1984, with a braid by John Dornan which had 12 rows slip. Further study of this same issue revealed another punchcard by John Dornan (from South Australia) called 'Smocking' which slips for ten rows. The card is for the electronic machine and the instructions suggest using either a single colour or a change of colour every ten rows.

The accompanying punchcard, for the standard 24-stitch punchcard machine, is only punched for eight rows slip. I realized that the standard gauge was capable of knitting the same number of rows as the electronic machine without problems. The tea-cosy pattern used by machine knitters for many years should also have pointed the way to developing this type of patterning. How near were we to discovering the potential of slip stitch? Perhaps we were not ready for the 'crumpled' look. There seems to be a natural progression of ideas which take time to evolve and reach the point where they have a separate identity. Ruched, ripple, bubble or blister stitches – call them what you will – appear to be the stitches of the 1980s.

Recent publication of a book by Susanna Lewis, *A Machine Knitter's Guide to Creating Fabrics*, has shown that work is being developed on these lines but by using mostly hand tooling. The effects are quite spectacular but do take a certain amount of application to master and are time-consuming. The technique I am working on is based on the punchcard. Once the punchcard design is understood it is possible to produce these bubble stitches, with the quilted look, on the Japanese single-bed machines, completely automatically.

# Yarn selection

Use one of the yarn combinations mentioned in Chapter 1 (*see Yarn guide*), making sure that it is no thicker than a 3-ply. Most machine knitters have large stocks of yarn which can be used for experimentation; anything will do. The colours do not matter too much at the beginning of sampling, as it is the effect which is of interest. If your machine knits without trouble with the selected weight of yarn there should be no difficulty later when knitting garments. There is a possibility that a garment will be too heavy when knitted in bubble stitch; hence the need for finer yarns if a jacket or sweater is to be knitted.

The Passap model books are the richest source of these ruched designs. Careful study of the Deco cards helps us to understand the principle of these fabrics.

### Designing petal slip stitch cards

The standard punchcard (24 or 30 stitches) is punched the opposite way to the Passap Deco card, i.e. the stitches which knit are punched, the slipped stitches are left blank. Using an eight-row pattern and the elongation button as a starting point it becomes obvious that to obtain the correct distortion of the fabric the blocks of slipped stitches have to be shunted along the punchcard by the width of the blocks of the slipped stitches, e.g. two stitches slipped means that on the next pattern change the block is two places to the left or right of the original selection (*Fig. 31*).

I have set out the progression of the design as a series of experiments showing how each stage developed. I suggest that you read through the various stages to enable you to have a full understanding of the punchcard. After seeing how the punchcard works it should be possible to use your own knowledge to expand the idea.

The punchcard in Fig. 33 was designed for the Fine Knitter to see whether the D could be mirror-imaged on the punchcard machines.

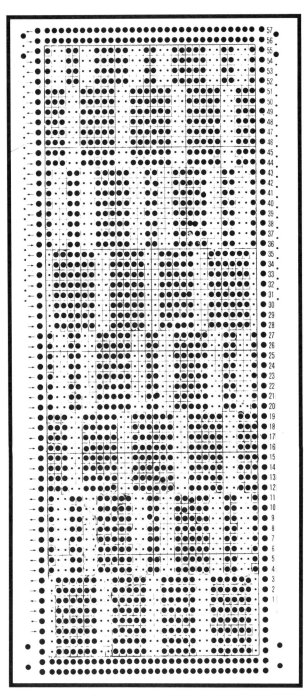

33 Petal slip stitch punchcard (fine knit)

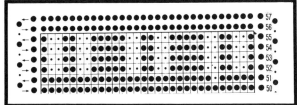

## KNITTING INSTRUCTIONS

1 Use a normal colour-change sequence:

16 rows colour 1.

16 rows colour 2.

16 rows colour 3.

Repeat throughout the card.

Figure 34 (top) shows the pattern produced by the punchcard after knitting. The petals outlined in this photograph form an interesting shape. In order to knit the shape the colour sequence has to be altered.

2 Altered colour-change sequence:

16 rows colour 1. RC16.

16 rows colour 2. RC32.

16 rows colour 3. RC48.

16 rows colour 2. RC64.

16 rows colour 1. RC 80.

Using the new sequence, the flower shape is revealed (Fig. 34, bottom). The order in which the colour is changed has completely altered the pattern produced by the same card. Changing colour on the correct row is vital. An incorrect colour change can completely alter the appearance of a design.

The section of the punchcard which intrigued me most was the flower shape. I decided to isolate this section as being the most interesting. It was necessary to return to the electronic machine to eliminate the tedious punching required for these designs.

3 Using the redesigned card (Fig. 35) on the standard-gauge machine and the altered colour-change sequence, knit at least two full patterns.

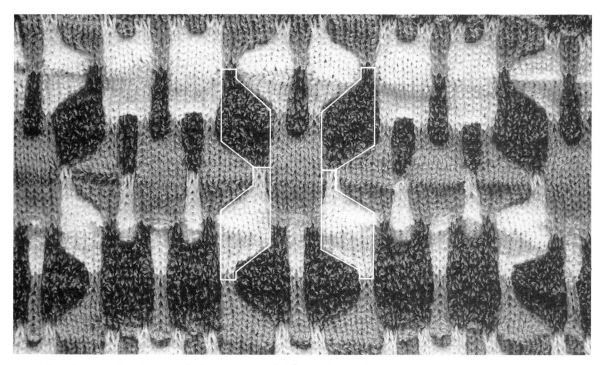

34 *Outline of a flower shape* (top) *and the flower shape revealed* (bottom)

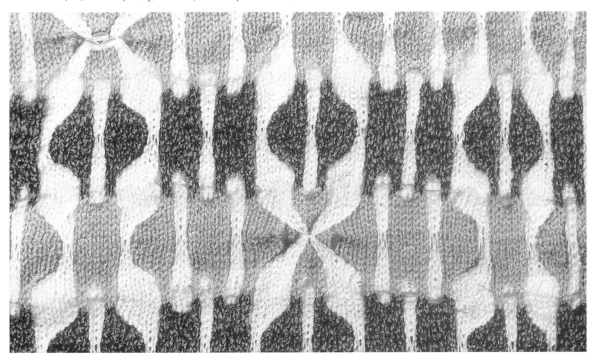

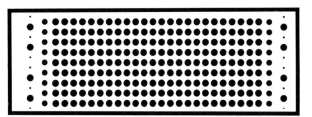

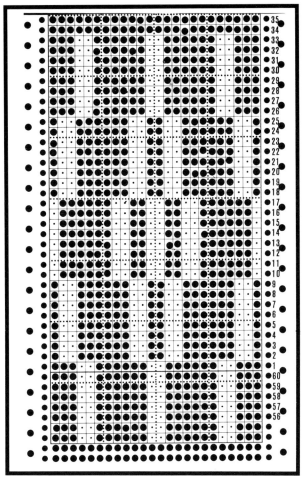

35 *Petal slip stitch punchcard (24 stitches)* (bottom)  *b Five-row extension* (top)

The simplified punchcard emphasizes the flowers, giving an appearance of quilted flowers set into the background (*Fig. 36, left*). The design has been adapted to 24 stitches for use on the standard punchcard machine. The 24-stitch pattern produces a larger, bolder flower effect which is quite pleasing.

4 If the flowers are separated by a few rows of stocking stitch, then the flowers are emphasized (*Fig. 36, right*). To avoid having to change the cams, punch out five full rows of holes on a spare piece of card. This is the easiest way of extending the design as the extension can be used or not, just as you please. It is possible to return the cam setting to stocking stitch but a few minutes spent punching the card will save you from the need to think of anything other than the colour change.

At this point I felt that the punchcard was fully developed. The flowers were isolated and had a definite quilted look and the added rows separated the lines of flowers. The design was different from anything I had knitted before and was worked without a change in the cam setting.

5 Whilst trying out a tension square using the punchcard with the stocking stitch rows, I felt it was time to select colours to knit a garment. To test the colour mix, two rows of each colour were knitted to see whether the colour blend was balanced and to check that the yarns were running freely. When the tension piece was released from the machine the six rows of colour had formed scallops. Would the scallops reverse if more plain rows were added to the end of the punchcard?

Knit in the same sequence as before to RC80 when all the needles will be selected:

Knit 2 rows in the centre colour yarn (CY).

Knit 2 rows in the background colour yarn (BY).

Knit 2 rows in the petal colour yarn (PY).

Knit 2 rows in the background colour yarn (BY).

Knit 2 rows in the centre colour yarn (CY).

The needles for the next repeat are selected on the last row of the band of stripes. The stripes add another point of interest as well as lightening the fabric (*colour plate 3*).

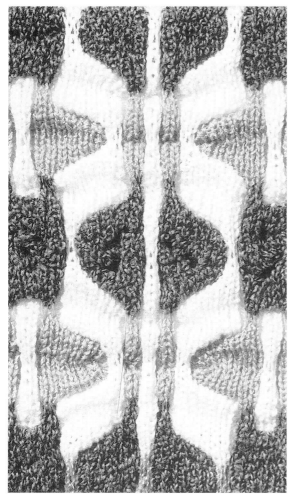

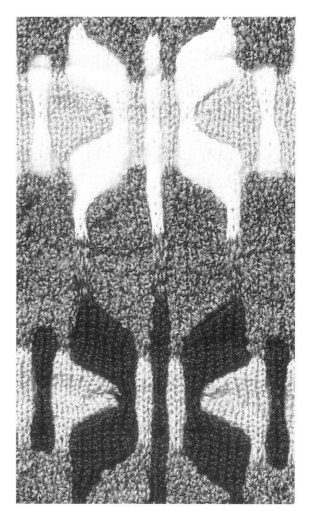

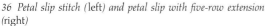
36 *Petal slip stitch (left) and petal slip with five-row extension (right)*

## VARIATIONS

1 A card can be punched for two rows with every hole punched. Copy rows 9–32 inclusive from the punchcard then punch two or more rows with every hole punched to produce flowers with rounded petals separated by a band of stocking stitch.

2 The pattern is rather formal. To alter the look it is possible to punch another card with the flowers shifted a few stitches along the row. Owners of electronic machines will not have to redraw the card, merely reprogramme the machine with the amended first needle position.

The above ideas are just to get you started on further development of this type of punchcard. The original idea, sparked off by a Passap stitch, has proved to be a most interesting exercise.

The way the design has evolved has produced an unusual look to slip stitch, giving it a new lease of life. The way the colour interlocks when knitting 16 rows

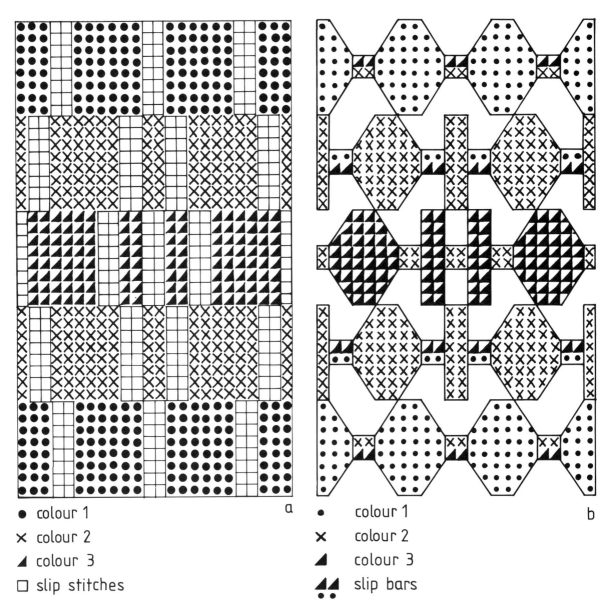

• colour 1                                    a
× colour 2
◢ colour 3
□ slip stitches

*37a Diagram of punchcard 35*

• colour 1                                    b
× colour 2
◢ colour 3
◢◢ slip bars
•  •

*b The knit rows collect behind the slipped stitches*

before a colour change made me realize that what we are actually knitting is an extended 'maze' pattern. Trying the previous experiments helps us to understand just what is happening with the colour blocks. The 16 rows of knitting have to settle somewhere. The fabric cannot spread out where the stitches are being slipped so they use the nearest open space,

which is the gap left by the slipped stitches of the previous 16 rows. We have seen that the colour-change sequence is of vital importance. What we are knitting using this method of slip is an illusion. It is difficult when looking at the fabric to realize that there is only one colour being knitted on any row. The fact that the slipped stitches have been held for

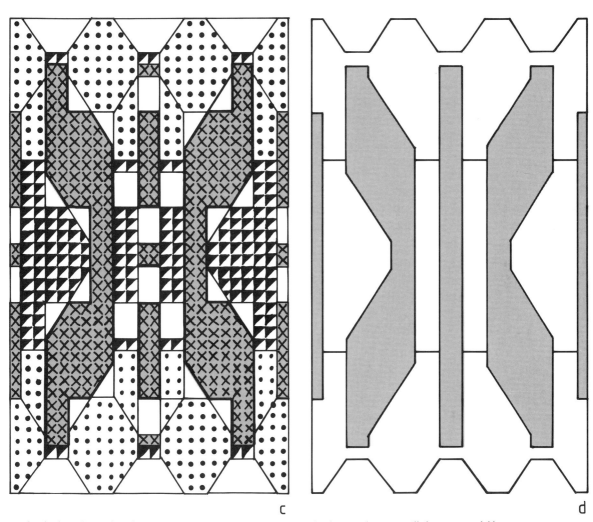

c  *The slip bars distort the fabric*

d  *The extra knit rows fill the space available*

so many rows creates the illusion that more than one colour is being used at a time. The slipped stitches of the previous block of colour drag the 16 rows being knitted into an area not usually available (*Fig. 37a–d*).

It is a fact that working for long periods of time on a design can cloud the mind. The brain seems only to see what it is looking for. New shapes and possibilities are ignored. To break the mental block it often needs a fresh eye. Someone not involved in the design can bring a new perspective. The jacket in colour plate 3 was completed and shown to a student who immediately said she could see butterflies. If you

look at the photograph carefully the shape is there but a couple of attempts to produce the motif were unsuccessful. Fate took a hand.

When one is working at home, adaptability is a great asset. An invasion of teenagers during the school holidays tends to disrupt the work pattern. I find this forced change an intrusion but the distractions can be creative! An ability to concentrate on work, give instructions on computer use and explain where to find a clean towel at the same time can make a contribution. The fact that a thought pattern is broken can lead to mistakes which become the turning point in the development of a design. Butterfly slip stitch was the result of such an interruption. Long after the idea was abandoned, the failure to change colour in the correct order showed the way. Unlike the deliberate alteration to the colour-change sequence in petal slip stitch, this development was a happy accident.

## BUTTERFLY SLIP STITCH

Using the punchcard in Fig. 35 and the same colour sequence as before, knit as follows until RC48:

16 rows BY. RC16.

16 rows PY. RC32.

16 rows CY. RC48.

After RC48 with COL the BY is then selected and used for the next 16 rows. Disconnect the punchcard, change to stocking stitch and knit a few rows.

As at the beginning of the experiments on petal slip stitch, the importance of changing colour in the correct place to obtain the pattern you are seeking is clearly illustrated.

The petal yarn becomes the bottom set of wings. The centre yarn becomes the top set of wings. There is no doubt that colour is important in any design but more so in this type of slip as we are creating an illusion of shape. Instead of the soft colourings used for the jacket, the butterfly needs to be in bold bright colours to emphasize the shape. Study pictures of butterflies and moths for inspiration. Brighter colours will make the butterflies seem even more real.

### VARIATIONS

1 Work the butterfly as instructed in the original design, placing beads in different positions on the wings.

2 Knit the butterfly as instructed in the original design to RC32. Knit 32 rows in the next colour for the second set of wings. This will mean turning back the punchcard on the 48th row to the beginning of the section (32 rows knitted with the same needle selection); RC64. The extra rows swirl around the area between the slip bands and push out the top wings to give them slightly more width than the bottom set of wings (*colour plate 4*). It is useful to test the theory before punching a card. If you decide to go ahead, the third section of the punchcard will have 16 rows.

It is amazing that a pure accident can result in such a spectacular change to a punchcard. We should be aiming at designing punchcards knowing how they will turn out rather than waiting for all these mistakes to occur. The best way to develop and use the knowledge gained by working through the various stages of the petal slip stitch experiment is to follow the diagrams of the punchcard in Fig. 37. If you use a different colour sequence the design emphasis alters the shapes quite dramatically.

Take a careful look at the knitted samples and try to relate the sections of knitting to the relevant section on the punchcard. This will enable you to manipulate the punchcard and produce the shape you want without waiting for a happy accident or mistake to occur. Whilst experimenting on another idea, I included a few rows of stocking stitch between the slip sections with fascinating results.

The standard punchcard has been interrupted with two blank rows at planned intervals. PP11E, marked for the electronic machine or the Passap because it is a 20-stitch design, is the result. The flowers, with six petals, are more natural and less stylized than the original petal slip stitch. The design is slightly more complicated to knit as we have, for the first time, to change the colour after a different number of rows. It is possible to try out the design by disconnecting the punchcard where the blank rows should be but the result of this idea is well worth the effort of punching a card.

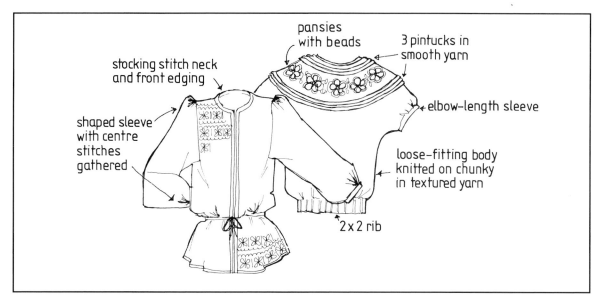

*38  Petal slip stitch jacket and yoked top*

## POPPY SEQUENCE

PP11E is 20 stitches wide. 24-stitch punchcard (*Fig. 100*).

Knit 7 rows stocking stitch in BY. COR.

Set your machine to memorize the pattern as before. Knit 1 row to set the memory. RC000 and proceed as follows:

Change to PY. Knit 16 rows, all needles selected.

Change to CY. Knit 4 rows, pattern selected on last row.

Change to PY. Knit 16 rows, all needles selected on last row.

Change to CY. Knit 4 rows, pattern selected on last row.

*Note*  The punchcard in Fig. 100 requires 20 rows of knitting in the PY sections.

Change to PY. Knit 16 rows, all needles selected on last row.

Change to BY. Knit 8 rows, pattern selected on last row.

Once memorized, the sequence is not too difficult. There are still only three colours: the background yarn, the petal yarn and the centre yarn. With machines which preselect, the petals – which are all the same colour – are knitted when a pattern is selected across the needlebed. As there are three sets of stocking stitch it is quite easy to see which colour to use. When all the needles are selected, a colour change to either the background yarn or the centre yarn is needed. There is no need for a cam change. For machines which do not preselect, see Chapter 3, page 37.

When a sample has been knitted and found to be more or less how you want it, it is time to use the correct colours. My aim was to produce poppies. The obvious colours to choose were red, black and green. The combination was stunning (*colour plate 5*).

On the second pattern repeat I shifted the first needle position six stitches along for a more informal look (PP43E is the alternative punchcard version). This is such a simple alteration but one which makes all the difference to the design. The poppy could perhaps be enhanced with a black bead in the centre of the flower; personally I prefer it unadorned. It is striking as it is, even though the six petals are not correct in botanical terms. With the development of the punchcard to the point where we have recognizable flowers instead of the stylized ones described at the beginning of the chapter, it seemed a pity to stop further development. Smaller flowers were the next step.

We moved away from the standard 16 rows slip when the punchcard was interrupted by the stocking stitch rows. By using 14 rows slip, two rows of stocking stitch and reducing the petal width to four stitches, a smaller flower is produced. This flower is not quite as realistic as the poppy but is nevertheless quite useful and of some interest as it adds another dimension to the collection. The trouble is that it is a 16-stitch repeat which can only be used on the electronic machine (PP12E). With the knowledge you have gained by following this chapter, if you have a 24-stitch repeat you could perhaps develop an adaptation which fits into this system. The design can be adapted quite easily to a 15-stitch repeat for the Fine Knitter.

Niggling away in the back of my mind was the need for a five-petalled flower: a pansy or a viola perhaps. It was quite simple to do this. Merely eliminating the centre block of slip was all it took. The first attempt produced a recognizable shape but the fifth petal was out of proportion. To correct this all that was needed was a slip band three stitches wide to reduce the number of stitches in the fifth petal (PP13E). Again the pattern is 16 stitches wide. Try working out an even smaller flower. Check whether 12 rows slip with petals which are three stitches wide will produce a recognizable flower. Figure 38 shows how petal slip stitch might be used in garments. See also Chapter 10 for pattern details.

# 5 Decorative trims

Most of the decorative trims we use are based on tuck stitch or lace. Slip has been used to knit cords and in double jacquard bands but, on the whole, it has been ignored. The obvious starting point for decorative trims is the loop braid by John Dornan mentioned in the previous chapter. The braid has a sculptured look, there are no floats and it is fully automatic (*Fig. 39a*) The potential for development of this trim became obvious as my knowledge of slip increased.

39a *Loop braid as an edging, PP14*
  b *Loop braid as an insert, PP14*
  c *Double braid, PP16*
  d *Curved loop braid, PP15*

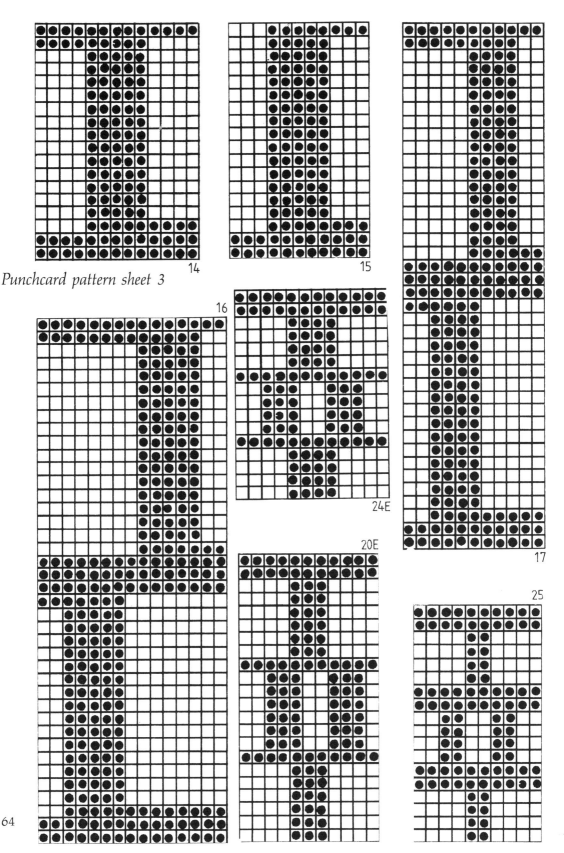

Punchcard pattern sheet 3

14  15  16  24E  20E  17  25

64

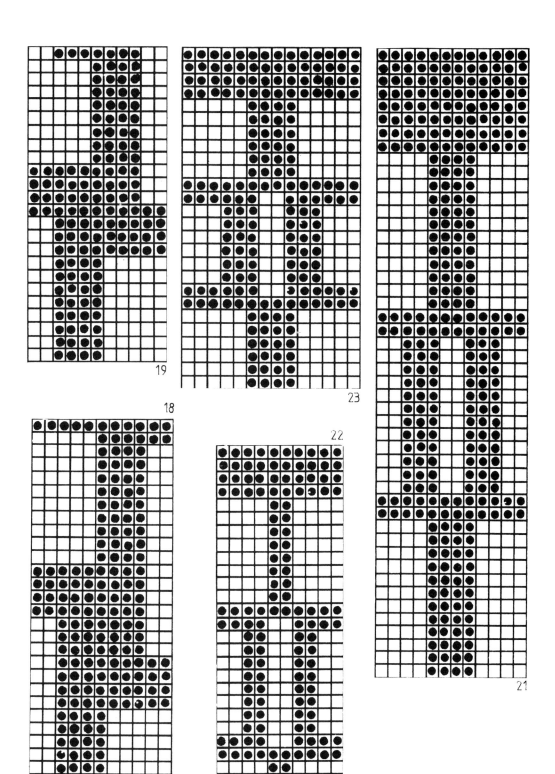

19

18

23

22

21

40a *Loop braid, PP17,*  b *loop braid, PP18,*  c *loop braid, PP19*

## LOOP BRAIDS

### KNITTING INSTRUCTIONS

#### Basic braid (*PP14*)

1  Cast on over 13 stitches. Knit a few rows in WY. COL.

2  Change to MY and knit 1 row. COR.

3  Set the machine to slip and to memorize the pattern. Knit 1 row to the left. All needles are selected.

4  Set the carriage to slip. Release the card and continue to knit. The needles are automatically selected and returned to their required positions by the punchcard.

### VARIATIONS

1  Use the braid as an insert by knitting over 9 stitches. This allows 2 stitches each side of every loop which is sufficient to hold the braid in shape. Any width can be knitted up to 13 stitches (*Fig. 39b*).

2  If the braid is to be used as an insert for a yoke, the card can be redrawn to knit more rows on one side of the braid than the other, thus knitting in an automatic curve (*PP15; Fig. 39c*).

By increasing or decreasing the width of the braid and altering the length of the loop, many variations are possible. The braid can be adapted to produce alternating loops on either side of the centre by using the full width of the basic braid. Each loop is marked on either the left or the right of the punchcard instead of the centre.

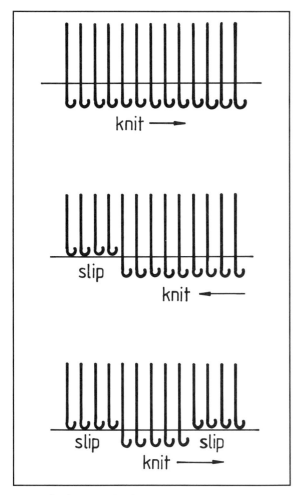

*41 Needle selection for braids*

## Designing loop braids

1 The most important point to remember when designing is that the card must be marked in such a way that those sections of the braid which need to slip must be put out of action at the opposite side to the carriage so that there will not be any floats formed by the yarn stranded across the back of the knitting (*Fig. 41*).

2 Each pattern must have an even number of rows.

3 Vary the number of stitches in each loop.

4 Vary the number of rows in each loop.

5 Overlap the centre stitches.

It does not take long to realize how many variations can be developed from this one idea. Using these ideas opens up the possibility of designing innumerable braids which can be knitted automatically, by punchcard, on every gauge of machine.

## FLOWER BRAIDS

After working on the looped braids and producing some surprising results the project was put aside. I had been unable to knit the braids in two or more colours without the introduced colour showing up in the background and felt that time would be better spent on other ideas.

The discovery, described in Chapter 4, that quite small flowers could be knitted using slip stitch in a full-width fabric, was a step forward but the possibility of using this technique in braids had not occurred to me. It was not until the purchase of a book of hand-knitting designs, *Stitches in Time* by Sue Bradley, that the concept of knitted flower braids came together.

One of the designs in the book has a trimming of woven flower braid. This braid set the bells ringing. Why should we have to search for an edging to match our knitwear when we already have the correct colours left over from the garment? Could we not knit the braid?

Use PP16 and knit in the same way as the basic braid. On the machine the braid looks strange but when it is released from the machine and pulled lengthways the knitting rolls over on itself to form the most interesting flat braid with loops on either side (*Fig. 39d*).

A few designs have been marked on punchcard pattern sheet 3 for you to try. Figure 40 (*PP17–19*) illustrates how each will turn out. Use these as a starting point to create your own loop braids. The most interesting ones occur where the centre stitches are working all the time.

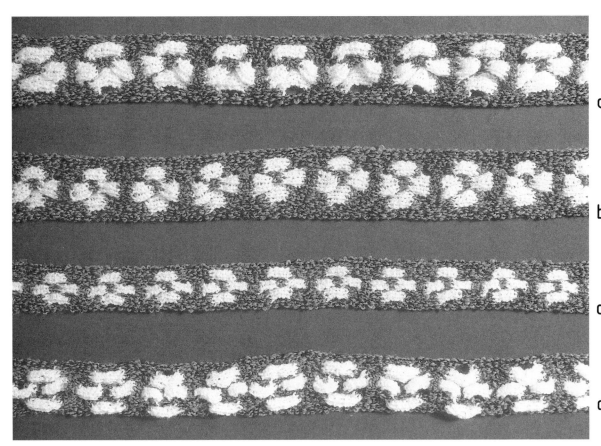

The knowledge that raised flowers could be knitted, albeit across the fabric, and that braids as wide as 15 stitches were successful, suggested that knitted flower braids were a possibility. In Chapter 4 I left you with a puzzle to solve. Was it possible to knit flowers even smaller than 16 stitches wide which fitted into a standard punchcard? Whilst working on another fabric I discovered how to knit cherries using a combination of stitches (*Fig. 85*). Once the cherries were designed the penny dropped and I was able to produce quite small flowers which, when knitted in fine yarn, result in beautiful narrow flower braids.

## KNITTING INSTRUCTIONS
### Basic flower braid (*PP20E*)

*Note* For details of punchcard marking, see Chapter 1.

*42a Flower braid, PP20E   b Flower braid, PP21   c Flower braid, PP23   d Flower braid, PP24E*

1 Cast on 12 stitches over the relevant needles. Knit a few rows in BY. COR.

2 Set machine to memorize 1st row of pattern. Knit 1 row. Release the card.

3 The centre three needles are selected. Change to flower colour (CY). Knit 12 rows.

4 Change to BY. Knit 2 rows.

5 Change to CY. Knit 12 rows.

6 Change to BY. Knit 2 rows.

7 Change to CY. Knit 12 rows.

8 Change to MY. Knit 4 rows.

The first flower is complete. Repeat steps 3–8 a few times to see the full effect (*Fig. 42a*).

What was most exciting was the fact there were no floats at the back of the braid. The flower colour was not visible anywhere in the background and because the flowers were only four rows apart, the strand of yarn from one to the other was not at all noticeable.

The twelve rows of knitting over two stitches elongated the petals and I felt that the flowers were being pushed out of shape. This could be due to the fact that I used a fine strand of cotton as the background yarn which was unable to hold the flower in shape. The braid was still quite interesting but did not produce the effect I was looking for. A thicker yarn for the background would more easily hold the shape of the flowers but would alter the character of the braid. This combination of thicker yarns was used in the dress in colour plate 10.

## VARIATIONS

Experiment with different yarns. Each combination will result in a braid with different emphasis.

1 With a fine yarn as the background the braid can be used with the edge stitches rolled under to show off the flower shapes.

2 With a slightly thicker yarn as the background the braid looks very interesting if used when opened out. Because each section of the braid is knitted independently, holes are formed in the fabric where the twelve rows are knitted over the two stitches. Opening out the braid reveals these holes to add another dimension and point of interest to the knitting.

3 The background yarn and the flower yarn are knitted independently. They only join where the background and flower petals meet. It is important to keep the yarns separate. The background yarn must be threaded to the left of the flower yarn to prevent them from tangling. As the colour is changed every few rows there is no reason why each flower cannot be a different colour. If you use a random dyed yarn, the flowers will shade through the colour spectrum.

The flowers could be knitted in a multitude of colours using a method suggested by Kaffe Fassett in his book *Glorious Knitting*. He suggests that short lengths of different tones of the same colour yarn are knotted together and knitted as the contrast yarn in a Fair Isle pattern. I see no reason why machine knitters cannot use the idea for petal slip stitch. It goes against the grain to have knots in the work but if you plan the colours beforehand and watch for the knots as they appear it is possible to hold the yarn down at the side to avoid knitting them in.

This type of knitting, with constant changes of colour, requires concentration. It is not difficult, however, and now that we have moved away from regular colour changes, a more steady knitting speed will produce better work more quickly, enabling us to spot the knots rather than knitting them in. Knit a sample to find out how much yarn is needed to knit a flower. When you have worked the sample, pull out the knitting and measure the length of yarn required for the flower section. Use this as a guide to cut lengths of different-coloured yarns.

The above ideas can be applied to a flower with any number of stitches and rows to each petal. Several different braids can be produced from PP20E. Each design is different from the others and will produce a braid with a similar look but with a distinct characteristic all its own. (*Fig. 42a–d*).

These braids will knit on the chunky machines but look better if half the number of stitches and rows are used. On the 155 with its 12-stitch pattern base, the original cards can be used. Select patterns which have only a few rows in each loop. The pattern cards are automatically halved as every alternate space on the pattern panel is blank.

*Punchcard pattern sheet 4*

Ruffles

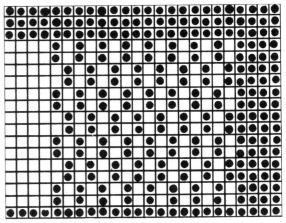

# RUFFLES

A ruffle is a piece of fabric which gathers into an attached straight edge. To obtain this edge ruffles have to be knitted sideways.

Once again we have to acknowledge the skill of the Australians who, in 1984, in the same article as the one with the loop braid, published a selection of ruffles on punchcards and mylar sheets. The ruffles in this section are adaptations and developments of their ideas.

## Basic ruffles

To find out how many rows are needed in the gathered sections of the ruffle it is a good idea to completely punch a card. If you look at PP26 the reason becomes obvious. Only three or four stitches at the left of the punchcard are left blank for 10–20 rows. It is easy to place sticky tape over these sections until you find the correct number of rows for the type of ruffle you are knitting. Remember to leave at least four rows fully punched between the blank sections. These four rows form the straight edge needed to attach the ruffle to the edge of the garment and to add length to the ruffle. (*Fig. 43, top*).

### KNITTING INSTRUCTIONS (*PP26*)

1 Cast on in WY and knit a few rows. COR.

2 Change to MY. Lock the card and knit 1 row to the left to memorize the pattern.

3 Release the card. Set the carriage to slip and continue knitting for the required length.

The four needles, not required for the gathered section of the ruffle, are held in slip position by the punchcard until they are needed. They then come forward to the knitting position, at the opposite side to the carriage to make sure that there are no slip bars across the work, and are knitted for four rows before being placed back into slip position ready for the gathered section of the ruffle.

43 *Basic ruffle, PP26 (top), vertical stripe, PP28 (centre) and mosaic pattern, PP29 (bottom)*

The markings are designed on a 24-stitch base which can be altered to any width less than 24 stitches on a standard punchcard, making it an extremely versatile card.

### VARIATIONS

The basic ruffle can be altered in a number of ways:

1 The number of rows in the gathered sections can be altered.

2 The width of the flounce can be altered. The method varies according to which machine you are using.

  a *Punchcard machines – any width from 10–24 stitches*

  To alter the width of the ruffle, cast on any number of stitches up to 24 anywhere on the needlebed, making sure that you are working on one of the 24-stitch sections of the needlebed which match the markings on the pattern panel *see Chapter 1, Punchcard information).*

  b *Electronics – any width from 10 stitches upwards*

  *Brother 910 and 950*

  Programme as an A + B pattern, using the last needle as pattern B.

  *Knitmaster 500 and 560*

  Mark the slip blocks only. Knit with button 1 right-hand light on. Button 2 right-hand light on. Place the needle 1 cam at the left of centre, the left-hand point cam behind this, the right-hand point cam 24 stitches away. Select the required number of needles at the right of this point cam. Any needles outside the point cam will knit because the negative button is in use.

  c *Passap – any width from 10 stitches to 40 stitches using the Deco*

  If the card is marked at the extreme left with slip sections then ruffles as wide as 40 stitches are possible. Remember to mark only half the number of rows you require. Use the Deco set to 2.

3 With the slip markings at the extreme edge of the punchcard it is possible to produce a trim with a centre spine of slip.

  By knitting the design as a single motif and including stitches on either side of the slip sections, a ruffle forms at each side of the centre.

4 An automatic rolled edge can be marked on the card by leaving the last two to four spaces at the extreme right of the card blank on every alternate row *(PP27)*. This is not possible on the Passap unless the ruffle is knitted using the BX setting and pushers, or the pushers are altered manually each time the lock is on the left.

Before marking a card with this edging try it out manually to see whether it produces the correct finish.

Follow the instructions for the basic ruffle but each time the carriage is on the right-hand side of the needlebed push the required edge stitches back to slip position. Alternatively place sticky tape over the relevant holes on the card.

The rolled edge, whether manual or automatic, is an excellent idea but it does have some drawbacks on the punchcard machines:

  a The width of the ruffle is restricted to the punchcard width.

  b The rolled edge could prove rather bulky if a thick yarn is used or the yarn cannot be damp-pressed.

  c The edge has only half the number of rows as the gathered part of the ruffle.

5 As there is no shaping in the gathered section of the ruffle, it is possible to knit a patterned fabric. Because the carriage is set to slip, any slip pattern which fits into the number of stitches and rows available can be used to knit the ruffle.

The ruffles have been designed with the slip sections on the left of the card which allows the colour changer to be used. The card is marked out in full because of the single line at the beginning of the pattern and the automatic hem. The two-colour pattern is designed on the same principle as the maze and mosaic patterns in Chapter 3.

**KNITTING INSTRUCTIONS (*PP28 OR PP29*)**

  1 Cast on in WY. Knit a few rows. COL.

  2 Change to CY. Set the machine to memorize the pattern and knit 1 row from left to right. All needles are selected. Release the card. Set the carriage to slip. Knit 1 row to the left.

  3 Change to MY. Knit 2 rows.

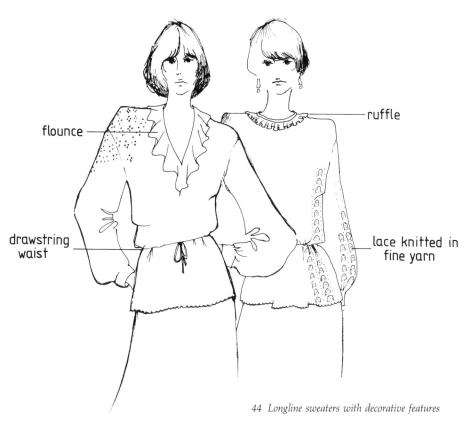

*44 Longline sweaters with decorative features*

Continue to change colour every 2 rows for the required length.

The two-colour idea works beautifully (*Fig. 43, centre*). The vertical stripes are broken up into panels by the full-width rows which were knitted with the same two-row sequence as the gathered sections.

If the gathered section of the ruffle is marked out with a number of rows which, when divided by two, produce an odd number of rows, i.e. 14 divided by 2 = 7, the coloured panels will alternate.

If the gathered section of the ruffle in PP28 is marked with a number of rows which, when divided by two, gives an even number of rows, i.e. 12 divided by 2 = 6, then the panels will stay the same colour.

The automatic rolled edge, used in section 4, forms a border of stripes in alternating colours. A bold stripe will be produced if the two to four edge stitches are marked on every row and the two-row colour sequence is used (*Fig. 43, bottom*).

The implications of the use of patterning with automatic shaping are quite fascinating, especially for punchcard machines. Although the method is restricted to the width of the pattern base it is useful to know that a simple and effective way has been found to introduce colour to a trimming, whilst shaping automatically, without having to change the cam setting or trying to remember to select certain needles to holding position. The electronic machines are again responsible for this advance. The idea needs more investigation on the electronic machines; up to now patterning and shaping, although possible, have been used separately, not in combination.

Figure 44 shows how various slip stitch decorative trims can be applied to fashion garments. (*See Chapter 10 for pattern details.*)

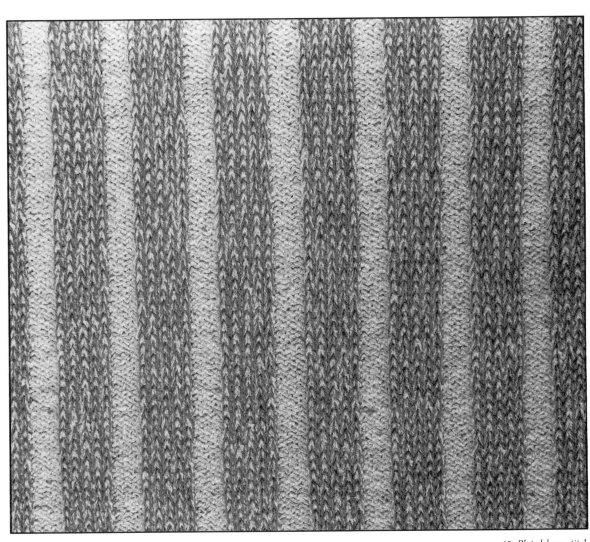

*45 Plated long stitch*

# 6 Double-bed slip stitch

There are many different ways of using the slip setting in conjunction with the ribber. Some of them overlap and could be said to belong in one or more sections. When using double-bed techniques I found it hard to remember whether the electronic machine had to be set to slip or double jacquard. To simplify things I have used the electronic machines as a guide. Where the electronic machine needs to be set to double jacquard or a special double jacquard card is needed to produce the correct finish, I have included it in Chapter 7. In this chapter the machine is set to slip for all the fabrics.

## LONG STITCH

Long stitch is a technique better known to Passap knitters. As our confidence in using a machine with a ribber has increased it has become more popular on the Japanese machines. The fabric that is created is extremely useful for straight skirts as it gives a ribbed effect without clinging (*Fig. 45*). When used in this way it is normally knitted in one colour. With the introduction of colour the fabric becomes double jacquard with long stitches over the whole surface (*see Fig. 59*).

Long stitch is formed over a two-row sequence. One row is formed by slipping the needles on one bed, for one row, whilst all the needles are working on the other. The slipped stitches are pulled up, to form long stitches, on the following row when all the needles knit on both the beds. The order in which the sequence is worked depends solely on the way the machine is set and which bed is patterning.

### KNITTING INSTRUCTIONS

#### Long stitch

1 Set ribber to half pitch. Cast on in FNR over required number of stitches.

2 After the circular rows have been knitted, transfer needles not required onto non-patterning bed. Gradually increase TD to 5/4. (On the patterning bed the tension needs to be higher than that on the plain bed.) Set patterning carriage to slip one way and knit the other, and the plain carriage to knit. Continue in this way for desired length.

A popular needle set-up is five needles in work, three out of work (*Fig. 46*). As it is non-selective, either bed can be used as the pattern bed. The stitch has been in use with various needle set-ups for a long time without much alteration. In *Passap Model Book 34* one design had a contrast colour stripe which disappeared behind the long-stitch stripes. This was achieved by slipping two rows on the pattern bed after the contrast colour stripe had been introduced.

The recent introduction of ribbers which can plate (the Brother 850 and the Knitmaster SRP 60N) has opened up new possibilities. With a fine yarn, in a contrast colour, in the plating feeder two-colour ribs

## Punchcard pattern sheet 5

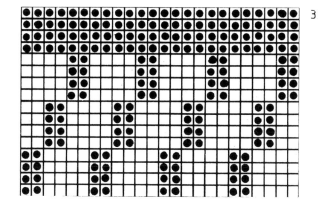

32

34

35E

36

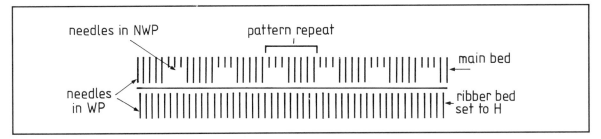

46 *Needle arrangement for long stitch*

can be knitted. Long stitch looks very attractive when knitted in this way (*Fig. 45*).

Pleats can be knitted if selected needles are taken out of work on each bed (*Fig. 47, bottom*). The top of the pleats can be stitched down or the skirt can be knitted to fit the hips and a stocking stitch basque added to reduce the bulk around the waist (*Fig. 47, top*).

## NON-SELECTIVE PINTUCKS

Pintucks knitted on the single bed are most attractive but they do entail a lot of hand work. Any number of rows can be knitted on the single-bed machine before the loops from the marker row are picked up and hooked onto the needles in work. A pintuck can be knitted automatically on the ribber but, on the Japanese machines, they can only be 4–6 rows deep depending on the yarn thickness.

The machine is set to slip and not to tuck as the name implies. Pintuck refers to a narrow fold or tuck in the fabric. Non-selective pintucks are a useful way of separating different pattern areas, especially if they are knitted in the same colours as the pattern.

47 *Needle arrangement* (bottom) *for plated long-stitch pleats* (top)

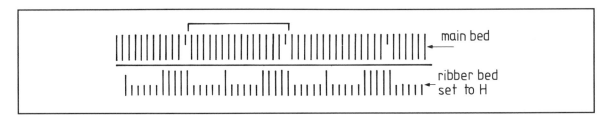

## KNITTING INSTRUCTIONS FOR RIBBER PINTUCKS

### Single-bed fabric

1 Knit garment as normal until pintuck section is reached. Lift ribber into place, set to half pitch and select required number of needles.

2 Select desired colour and, with main bed tension set as for the garment knitting and ribber tension set to 1, knit 1 row. COR.

3 Insert comb and weights, * set ribber carriage to slip and knit 6 rows. On 5th and 6th rows check carefully to see that all stitches on main bed have knitted off. COR.

4 Set ribber carriage to knit, knit 1 row in FNR. The first pintuck has been formed. COL.

5 Change colour if desired. Knit 1 row in FNR. **

Repeat from * to ** until the correct number of pintucks have been knitted. Transfer the ribber stitches to the main bed and continue to knit the garment. A ribber transfer carriage can be used to transfer the stitches to the main bed but do watch out for dropped stitches – otherwise the pintuck will have a droop where the stitch was dropped.

### Double-bed fabric

Double-bed pintucks are knitted in exactly the same way as those incorporated into a single-bed fabric except that the ribber is already in place and there is no need to transfer stitches to the main bed after each sequence of pleats.

The yoked top in Fig. 38 (pattern details, *Fig. 102*) has ribber pintucks to outline a yoke. The rest of the garment was knitted on the single bed. Ribber pintucks always lie the same way. If they are to be incorporated into a sideways-knitted garment with a centre pattern panel (*Fig. 48a*) then the second half of

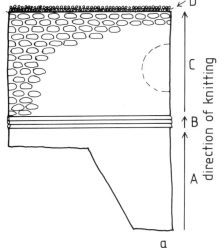

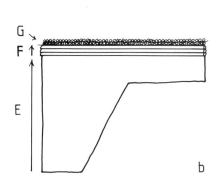

*48 Sideways-knitted sweater: a First section   b Second section c The two sections joined*

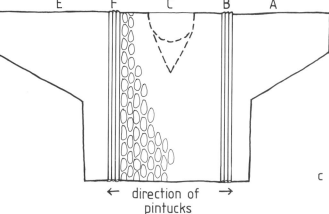

79

the garment will have to be knitted from the cuff to the centre with the pintucks added at the end of the piece in order that each set of tucks is facing the opposite way (*Fig. 48b*).

## SELECTIVE PINTUCKS

The pintucks we have used up to now have been non-selective. It is possible to knit textured fabrics with quite intricate pintuck effects by using a punchcard. The tucks are not in straight lines but undulate across the fabric depending on the punchcard pattern; neither are they true pintucks.

## Punch pintuck

Punch pintuck uses a punchcard to produce a single colour, double-bed fabric with a textured surface (*Fig. 49*). The pattern (*PP30*), formed by selected groups of needles knitting fewer rows on the patterning bed than on the plain bed, shows on the wrong (ribber) side of the fabric, and consequently a larger stitch size than usual is needed on the non-patterning second bed. The punchcard was tested on the electronic machine with the relevant markings but knitted as if it was a standard machine. I liked the effect. If you would like to reproduce the same effect as the sample, punch the card in reverse.

The technique is mentioned in the Passap manual using card 16 and in the Knitmaster ribber manuals

*49 Punch pintuck*

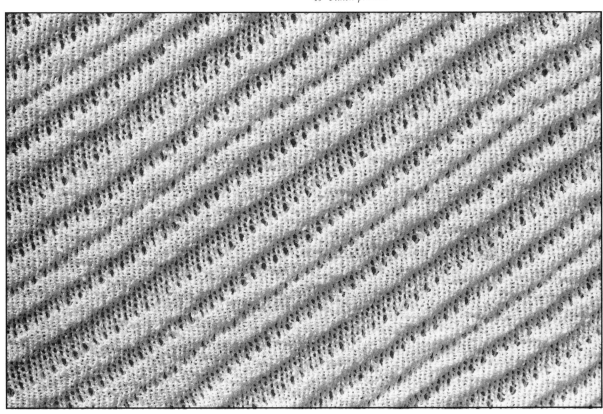

(cards 9 R–2 and 10 R–2 on the SRP 60N). Any machine with a ribber can make use of the technique to produce a fabric used by the knitwear industry in the production of classic pure wool jackets which command a high price in exclusive boutiques. Try Forsells 2-ply yarn to reproduce a similar effect.

## Two-colour pintucks

It is possible to knit multicoloured, textured fabrics which are based on pintucks. Once again it is the Passap which leads the way. The Passap is a double-bed machine and must be used as such even when knitting single-bed fabrics. At first the pushers and the two-colour changer were the only means of

50 *Two-colour pintuck*

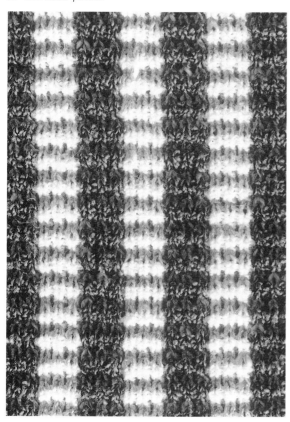

patterning. After the introduction of the four-colour changer and the Deco pattern system the fabrics produced by the Passap reached new heights.

Selective pintucks are a fairly recent development which combine the use of the colour changer and the ability of machines to knit a number of rows on one bed whilst stitches are held on the other. This technique is possible on the Japanese machines but fewer rows can be knitted on the patterning bed than on the Passap. The effect is still fascinating.

Kathleen Kinder illustrated the use of colour in pintucks in *The Machine Knitter's Book of the Ribber*, Volume 2, using Japanese machines. The different colours in the pintucks are selected by punchcard. The card needs to be marked so that every stitch in each sequence is marked; otherwise the stitch will not be knitted off and will cause the carriage to jam. Any more than two colours in a row could lead to problems as there will be floats behind each colour which will be enclosed when the next full needle rib row is knitted.

Two colours in a row would normally be knitted using the Fair Isle setting on the single bed but, as we are knitting with both beds, slip has to be used. (The Fair Isle setting cannot be used when the ribber arm is connected.)

Blocks of colour are most effective (*Fig. 50*). Anything more elaborate would be completely lost in the pintuck. PP31 and PP32 are examples of two- and three-colour pintucks. Do make sure that the ribber is set to slip when knitting the two-colour pattern and that the yarn is at the left when the colour is to be changed.

## Ripple stitch

The idea of two-colour pintucks was expanded by Susanna Lewis. Susanna has knitted a two-colour fabric with a flat, ribber background and pintucked pattern sections and has called the fabric 'ripple stitch', a perfect description (*Fig. 51, bottom*).

The method entails locking the punchcard, on selected rows, and knitting numerous rows on one bed before releasing the card. This is ideal when testing designs but if it is to be repeated over a whole garment then it is worth punching a card.

A card which I found in a Passap model book has been adapted to 24 stitches. Figure 51 (*top*) shows the original design after it was altered to 24 stitches but before it was marked to knit ripple stitch. The card is PP33. (PP34 is another ripple stitch pattern.)

## KNITTING INSTRUCTIONS

1 Cast on in FNR over 30/30 stitches on each bed in MY.

2 Increase tension gradually to 6/4. COR. Knit 1 row to memorize the pattern. COL.

3 Change to CY. Set ribber carriage to slip both ways. Knit 6 rows.

4 Change to MY. Alter ribber carriage to normal. Knit 2 rows.

Continue in this way for at least two full patterns (*Fig. 51, bottom*).

## Pattern notes

1 To ease the knitting, two full rows are punched so that the only cam change is on the ribber.

*51 Ripple stitch (bottom) and 24-stitch adaptation for ripple stitch (top)*

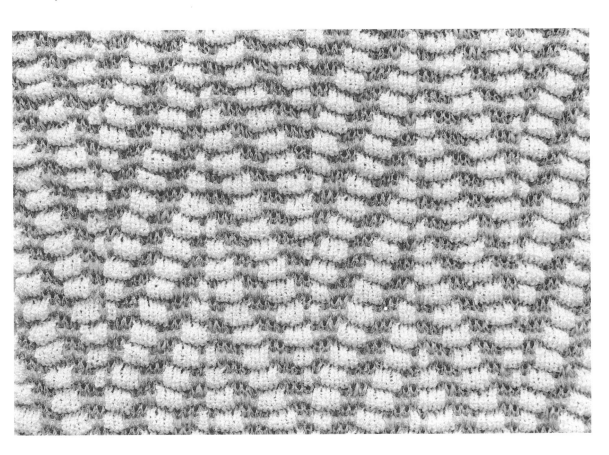

2 The tension on the Brother 950 needs to be 6/4; on the Knitmaster 560 it needs to be 7/5. (The main bed tension needs to be as near as possible to the normal stocking stitch tension.)

3 Use the side weights to prevent the slip bars from coming too far forward on the needles. Otherwise, when the next two rows of full needle rib are knitted, the ribber needles will catch and cause the carriage to jam. A slightly larger stitch on the ribber will allow the six extra rows to slot between the two beds, but do make sure that the ribber is not set to too high a tension as the full needle rib rows and the ribber stitches provide stability to the fabric. Too high a tension would produce a loose, floppy fabric with the enclosed floats showing through from the inside.

On the Knitmaster the stitches do not come forward whilst the pattern is being knitted because of the way the machine selects the pattern. They do come forward when the first full needle rib row is knitted.

There are a few ways of overcoming this problem.

a Bring forward to holding position a few needles on the left of the needlebed.

b Use side weights.

c Pull down the work until the row has started to knit.

4 The automatic cam change on the SRP 60N ribber can only be used when a small number of stitches are in working position. If the fabric width means that the carriage has to enter the colour-change area every alternate row, the drive lever will have to be lowered when the six rows are knitted. In this case the autoset lever cannot be used either as it trips the cams in the middle of the pintuck sequence. The cam change will have to be done by hand.

Ripple stitch and pintucks are an indication that interesting fabrics are possible when both beds are used selectively. Ripple stitch in particular, by the way it allows us to isolate certain sections and knit extra rows on one bed only, is similar to blister stitch (*see Chapter 7*). Blister stitch is produced by using the double jacquard method of knitting. The patterned section has smooth blisters instead of the ridged sections characteristic of ripple stitch.

# RELEASE STITCH

Release stitch makes use of the second bed in an unusual way. One bed has every needle in work and the second bed, either the ribber or the main bed, has certain needles selected to knit. The simplest release stitch pattern is to select groups of needles on the ribber, knit a few rows then rack and repeat. The stitches on the patterning bed are released before the stitches on the main bed are cast off (*Fig. 52, left*).

## KNITTING INSTRUCTIONS

1 Cast on every needle on the main bed. Push three needles to WP. Leave three in NWP along the ribber bed.

2 Knit a few rows over both beds. Rack three places to the left or right.

3 Knit a few rows over both beds and return the ribber to its original position.

Repeat steps 2 and 3 for the required length. Before casting off on the main bed, release the ribber stitches and allow them to unravel to the beginning of the knitting. Bubbles of loose stitches surrounded by sections of normal-size stitches are formed.

## VARIATIONS

### Using the basic setting

1 Rack the ribber one place to the left or right. Knit 2 rows, rack the ribber in the same direction, knit 2 rows. Do this at least 5 times (10 rows), then reverse racking until ribber is back in its original position.

2 Instead of releasing all the stitches, select the centre of each group and allow the stitch to run down (*Fig. 52, right*).

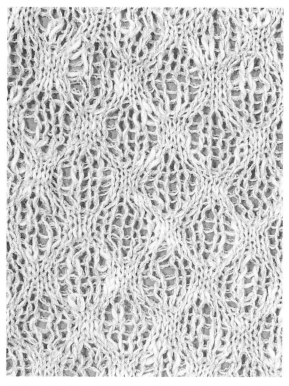

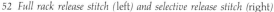

*52 Full rack release stitch (left) and selective release stitch (right)*

The fabric produced in variation 2 is the nearest we can get to combining lace-like effects with plain and purl stitches. The recent interest in Barbara Walker's three *Treasuries of Knitting Patterns* has once more highlighted the beautiful textures produced by such stitch combinations, one technique not available to machine knitters as yet. This last variation leads us on to selective release stitch used in conjunction with punchcards.

## Selective release stitch

Using the ribber as the patterning bed does have its restrictions. If the main bed becomes the patterning bed then punchcards can be used (*PP35E*). So far the stitches have been released at the end of the knitting as the groups of needles are constantly in use (*Fig.*

53a). With punchcard release stitch the groups of needles selected can change completely (*Fig. 53b*). The stitches from each section must be released before the next selection takes place. If this is not done then there will be a muddle as the released stitches will run into the plain sections below.

This type of release stitch is similar to drive and mesh lace (*see below*). The difference is that blocks of stitches are released at intervals whereas with drive and mesh lace the stitches are released every two rows.

## Knitmaster specials

The techniques which follow involve dropping or releasing stitches in a controlled manner to form lace-like patterns using a second knitting bed for the

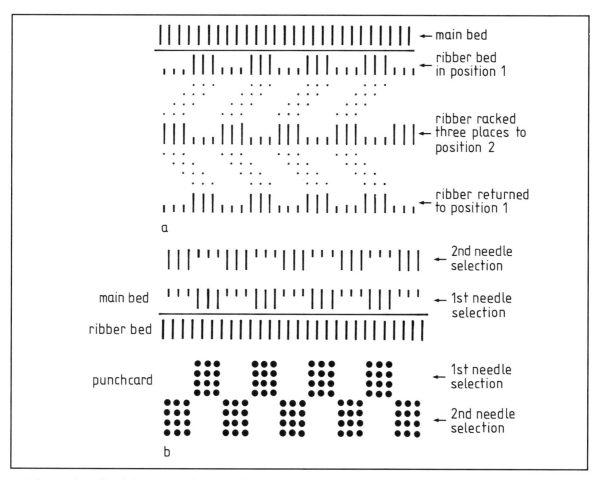

main bed

ribber bed
in position 1

ribber racked
three places to
position 2

ribber returned
to position 1

a

2nd needle
selection

main bed — 1st needle
selection

ribber bed

punchcard — 1st needle
selection

2nd needle
selection

b

53 *Release stitch: a Ribber-bed patterning   b Main-bed patterning*

pattern stitches. The technique can be worked on other machines but not with the same ease as on the Knitmaster.

Knitmaster ribbers are supplied with a P carriage which speeds up the stitch release. The P carriage is a standard accessory for the Knitmaster ribbers. Its purpose is twofold:

1 To bring to upper working position the needles on either bed to prevent them dropping.

2 To release stitches from the needlebed in two movements which speeds up and simplifies the knitting of drive lace, mesh lace, release stitch and pile knitting.

The P carriage is non-selective. Therefore any needles with stitches will be emptied by the P carriage.

## Drive and mesh lace

Drive lace and mesh lace are types of release stitch which use the ribber bed as the main bed. The pattern is knitted on the top bed in order to make use of the punchcard. After each row is knitted the stitches from the pattern needles are removed by the P carriage. They drop and form holes in the stocking stitch

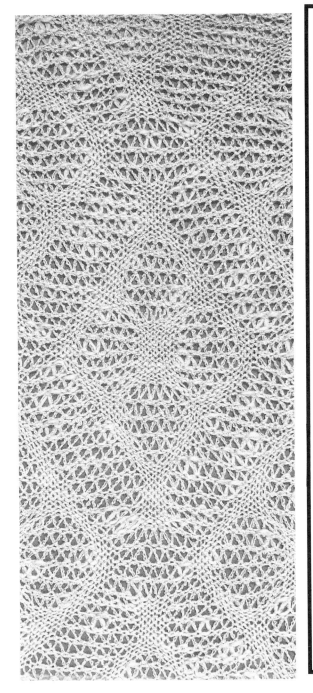

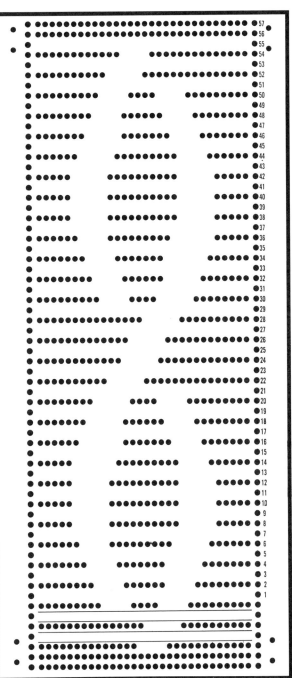

54 *Mesh lace*

55 *Ribber card for pile knitting (courtesy Knitmaster)*

which is being knitted on the ribber. The technique is simple to work on the Knitmaster because of the P carriage.

Drive lace is used to outline a shape as opposed to mesh lace which produces a mesh fabric which is outlined by stocking stitch. Figure 54 is a sample of an attractive mesh lace design from the 560 manual. It is a 30-stitch repeat. PP36 is a 24-stitch pattern of a similar type.

## PILE KNITTING

Pile knitting is a looped fabric that is produced very easily on the Knitmaster machines. The ribber arm is threaded with two fine yarns, one in the normal feeder and the second in the P feeder at the front of the ribber arm. The pile is knitted by the yarn in the main feeder. Both yarns knit on the ribber. The loops are locked when a second row is knitted on the ribber only.

The accepted method of marking cards for pile knitting is to have a blank row between each row of loops (*Fig. 55*). The punchcards for mesh lace and drive lace are interchangeable with those for pile knitting. The fabric is most effective. The looped pattern stands proud of the background. The yarn used for sampling was Astrakan and one end of fine cotton. The yarns were used in turn as either the loop yarn or the background yarn. The tension with Astrakan as the loop yarn was 6/4. The fine yarn as the loop yarn needed a tension of 5/4. Overall I preferred the loops knitted in Astrakan as the fabric looked more like towelling. Another way is to knit loops and release them with the P carriage every row. This produces a wider, denser fabric which is also extremely easy to knit. It eliminates the need to work out special punchcards, as ordinary Fair Isle patterns can be used. The instructions in the manual suggest that the P carriage is used on the ribber, to lift the stitches to upper working position before the next sequence is knitted. I did not find this necessary.

It is possible to knit pile knitting in two colours. I first saw the method in the Knitmaster section of *Creative Dressing* by Kaori O'Connor. Since this technique was introduced the YC6 colour changer has simplified the yarn change. The background yarn is now caught in the hook which is cut out of the yarn holder plate (*Fig. 56*), preventing it from becoming tangled with the yarn hooks.

Additional cards for Knitmaster mesh lace and pile knitting can be found in the Brother pattern book for the automatic garter carriage. This book had been on my shelf for well over a year before I realized that the cards were interchangeable. Conversely if you own a garter carriage the mesh lace and pile knitting cards can be used as a fresh source of patterns.

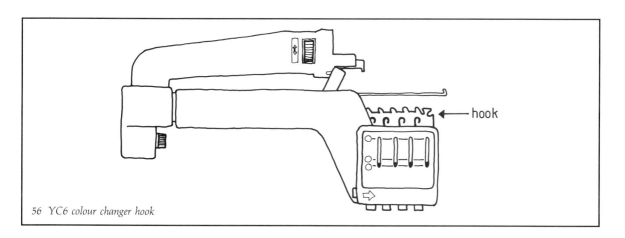

56 YC6 colour changer hook

← hook

87

# THREE COLOURS IN A ROW

In Chapter 3 we discussed using three or more colours in a row to produce a multicoloured Fair Isle effect. The floats which form when using this method of knitting are not really practical when being used for garments. The only way to eliminate the floats is to knit the same punchcard using the double bed to take up the floats. Passap knitters are quite familiar with this method of working. Card 20, in the basic pack, is ready punched for all-over three-colours-in-a-row slip.

In the Passap model books, particularly number 37, there are more examples of all-over multicoloured slip knitting, some with many more than three colours.

There are various ways of finishing the backing.

1 The Passap method for multicolour double-bed slip uses the bird's eye (1 × 1) setting on the non-patterning bed. Brother 850 owners can use this method as well.

This backing produces a fabric slightly thicker and more solid than ordinary double jacquard. The tension dial on the Brother 850 needs to be MB6/RB5. Even though the yarn I used was not too thick and the tension was set quite high, the density of the fabric was surprising.

The thickness of the fabric can be altered by changing the tension dial. Using the above tension there is no show-through which suggests that the tension can be loosened without spoiling the clarity of the pattern. As the machine is set to elongation, the pattern is slightly longer than the original design but is quite well proportioned because of the 1 × 1 backing which helps to widen the fabric and shorten the pattern. Tightening the tension will make a heavier, tighter fabric.

2 The ribber is set to knit every row. Consequently there are three times as many rows on the ribber as on the main bed which form pintucks on the wrong side. The fabric can be very firm and heavy but there are interesting possibilities if a feature is made of the

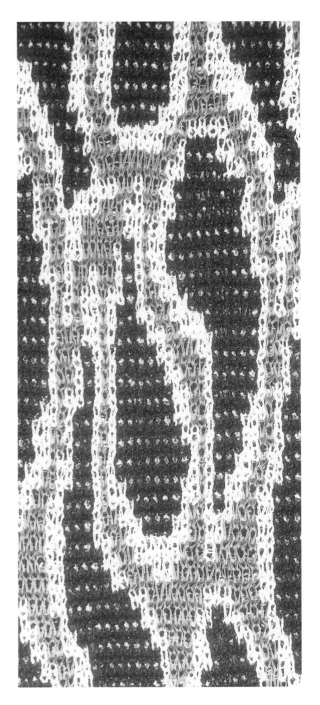

57 *Three colours in a row, knit side*

pintucks. The fabric is reversible: the knit side is patterned, the ribber side is pintucked (*Fig. 57 and colour plate 6*).

The Passap is used without weights which makes the fabric compact with deep pintucks. The Japanese machines use a comb and weights to produce a ribber fabric which tends to stretch pintucks. They will never be able to produce the same 'crunch' as that produced by the weightless machines but, by playing about with the yarn thickness and the tension dial, a similar texture can be reproduced.

The tension is most important. With the ribber knitting on a loose tension and the main bed knitting on a tighter one I found that the main bed was not knitting the stitches off the needles. To overcome this the close knit bar was inserted, enabling the tension to be set at 2/5 on the Brother 950/850. The fabric was knitted without problems.

Figure 57 is an example of a fabric with too loose a tension. The pintuck colours show through the knitting. Colour plate 6 shows a fabric produced by selecting the correct tension.

The pintucks were certainly more obvious with a definite ridging on the ribber side. After steaming the fabric I found that it was still quite supple and pleasing to the touch.

3 The ribber is set to slip one way and knit the other way, which is the accepted method of producing double-bed, three-colours-in-a-row slip. The fabric is not as heavy as with method 2 but there are still a lot of rows to fit into the fabric. Do not forget that floats are formed when the ribber slips a row. These will be enclosed by the next ribber row when it is knitted.

This is a more practical fabric as the thickness is reduced substantially despite the fact that the floats are enclosed. It is not as exciting on the ribber side as some of the previous methods but, if it is the pattern with which you are concerned, this is closer to the normal proportions of the design than either of the other methods.

4 Leave every alternate needle on the ribber out of work. There are many possible combinations to be used with this needle setting on the ribber. You may wish to knit every row or slip every alternate row; the

drop shoulder

three-colours-in-a-row jacquard

pintucks on the inside

58 *Drop-shoulder jacket*

choice is yours. The general effect will be the same as method 2 or 3 but the fabric and the pattern will be narrower and less bulky. The floats which are enclosed in the fabric are visible on the purl side of the knitting but they are held in place by the ribber stitches.

Fig. 58 illustrates the ideal garment shape for this type of fabric. Most of these fabrics require frequent colour changes and a simple garment with little or no shaping allows the knitter to concentrate on the knitting.

Each one of the above fabrics has its uses. One of the secrets of good design is to select the correct fabric for the correct garment. It is no good making a casual outdoor jacket in a droopy fabric with lots of floats or an evening jacket which is heavy and stiff.

Careful selection of yarns can alter the weight and texture of a fabric to a limited extent but if you have failed to select the correct fabric finish for the garment you are knitting, it is doubtful whether it will ever look right.

I believe, however, in breaking the rules if it suits me but you must know the rules before you can do this. The best way to find out which yarns produce which fabric, and which backing looks best with the various punchcards, is to sit down at the machine and try all the combinations. The knowledge you will gain from this exercise will stand you in good stead in the future. In time you will be able to spot immediately that certain yarn and stitch combinations just will not work. When you reach this stage you will be making and breaking the rules.

The yarns used throughout this experiment were Hobby with one strand of 2/30s Bright Acrylic in three different colours.

## KNITTING INSTRUCTIONS

### For double-bed three-colour slip

1 Cast on in FNR. Knit 2 rows in each colour to check that the yarn is set up correctly.

2 Knit to the right with colour 3. Lock the card on row 1. Set your machine to memorize the pattern, select one of the above ribber settings. Knit 1 row to the left.

3 Begin the pattern with colour 1. Knit 2 rows of each colour with the carriage set to slip and the machine to elongation, just as you did in Chapter 3 for the single-bed method. The only difference is that you have the ribber connected to take care of all the floats.

*Punchcard pattern sheet 6*

# 7 Double jacquard

## DOUBLE JACQUARD

Double jacquard is a floatless, patterned fabric produced on a double-bed machine. The technique was confined to industrial machines and the semi-industrial Passap until the mid 1970s when Knitmaster introduced a colour changer for their machines. My first introduction to the technique was in Mary Weavers book *The Ribbing Attachment*, Part 2. At the time it seemed incredible that floatless fabrics could be produced so easily. However, as there were not many fine yarns available the fabric produced was rather like cardboard. It is incredible to think how far we have advanced since then. With the advent of the new ribbers, the Knitmaster SRP 60N, the Brother 850, the Simulknit from Toyota and the availability of numerous fine yarns, many interesting textured fabrics are possible.

Basic jacquard is produced by setting the main carriage to slip and knitting each colour individually for two rows. The use of the slip setting combined with the ribber ensures that there are no loose floats on the wrong side of the fabric.

The colour is changed every two rows. After the initial row, which sets up the pattern, the first two rows are the contrast or pattern rows. The second two rows are the background or plain rows. Each four-row sequence means that two actual rows are knitted. The ribber knits the yarn which would be the floats in single-bed Fair Isle. There are several types of double jacquard which rely mainly on the different ways the ribber is set up. Each produces a different look to the patterned surface.

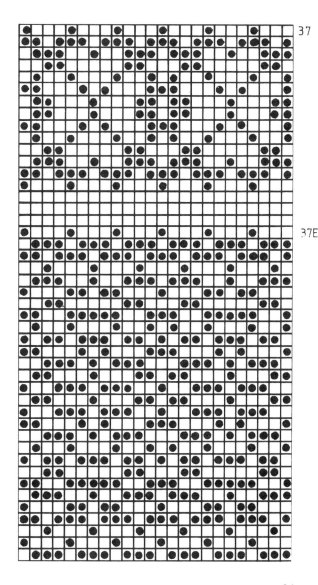

37

37E

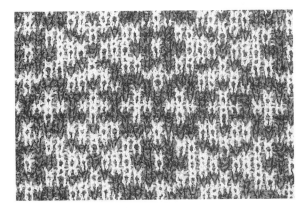

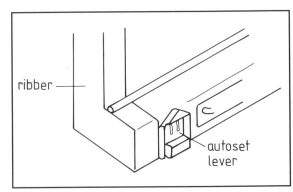

60 Autoset lever, Knitmaster SRP60N

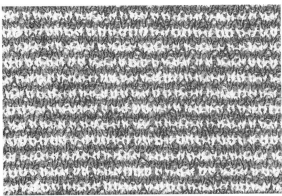

59 Double jacquard: knit side (top) and purl side (bottom)

## Striper jacquard

All needles are in work on both beds. The ribber is set to knit every stitch every row. The backing is in two-row stripes. The pattern is elongated (*Fig. 59 and colour plate 7*).

## Bird's-eye jacquard

Every needle is in work on both beds but the ribber carriage is set so that every alternate needle knits on alternate rows, the backing is speckled and the pattern is condensed. (This is only possible on Passap and Brother 850. The Brother 850 must have an even number of stitches to allow the needles to alternate.)

## Single-colour backing

By altering the ribber setting every two rows a single-colour backing can be produced.

The autoset lever at the extreme left of the needlebed on the Knitmaster SRP 60N ribber produces this backing semi-automatically by tripping the drive lever each time the carriage passes to the extreme left (*Fig. 60*).

The Toyota Simulknit differs slightly from the other ribbers as the two colours are knitted together in one row as in single-bed Fair Isle whilst simultaneously the ribber knits the fine yarn in the contrast feeder. The same backing is achieved automatically on the Passap by using BX and an arrow key on the back bed (*Fig. 61*).

Double jacquard is usually knitted in fine yarns. This is necessary because every needle on each bed is in work. To use any yarn thicker than 2-ply for the

61 Passap bird's-eye backing

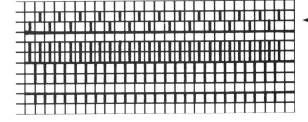

standard set-up could strain the machine. Using a 2-ply yarn with every needle in work produces a fabric the thickness of 4-ply, which is adequate for most needs.

First attempts at knitting double jacquard are not always encouraging. A lack of confidence in moving the carriage, threading the colour changer and changing the yarn can lead to tangled threads which, because they are so fine, tend to snap very easily. This often means the whole piece of fabric falls to the floor. If this happens, do not be too discouraged – cast on immediately, reset the machine and begin to knit again.

Most ribbing, once stitches have been dropped, is hard to pick up. Mistakes can be rectified but are time-consuming. It is quicker and easier to begin again if more than two or three stitches are dropped. 'Practice makes perfect' is a true statement when applied to any new knitting technique but never more so than when learning to use both knitting beds at once, the colour changer and the double jacquard setting. Familiarity with the way the punchcard works, which line in the pattern you have reached and which colour is to be knitted next will all help to give you the confidence needed to knit double jacquard with ease.

There is a lot to be learned from mistakes. If everything goes right from the beginning, all well and good, but if, when you have gone wrong, you realize why you did then this knowledge can be put to use later when working on more advanced

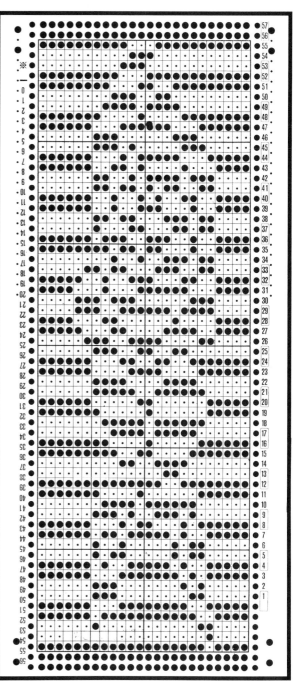

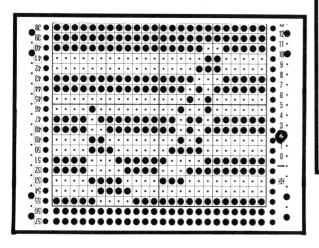

62 *Double jacquard punchcard*

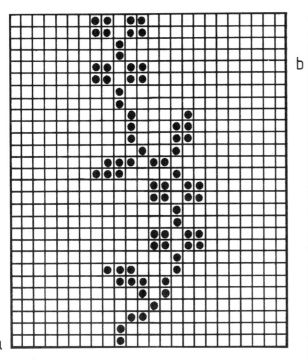

a

63 Double jacquard conversion: a Fair Isle design    b Pattern marked for double jacquard    c Complete card with background marking

b

methods and adaptations of double jacquard. Double jacquard is a very satisfactory way to produce a fabric. The sense of achievement when the first perfect piece of fabric is taken from the machine is second to none.

Double jacquard requires cards which have been specially punched (*Fig. 62*). To begin with it is easier to use the cards which come with your colour changer. If they are not supplied then you will have to punch your own. Although full details are given in the colour changer manuals, Fig. 63 shows, in diagram form, how to convert punchcards to double jacquard. The pattern in the example is an adaptation of Brother prepunched card 512. In previous chapters we have separated colours so that each has a row to itself. A similar method is used for double jacquard except that after the first row of background colour each colour must be marked for two rows as the rows may not be identical.

To ensure that the card is correct, check that in every two-row sequence all 24 spaces are marked. As

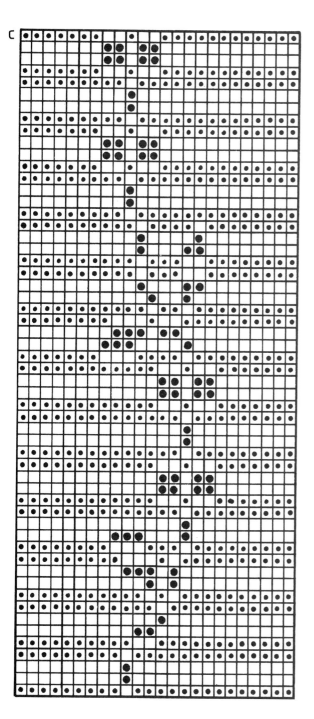

with three colours in a row, each stitch has to be knitted in one of the two colours.

Electronic machines do not need special cards. Any Fair Isle design is automatically converted to double jacquard by selecting the setting which is built into the machine. Since I bought my electronic machine I have used double jacquard frequently. The joy of flicking a switch to produce the fabric is hard to beat. Any design with long floats is easily and quickly knitted with this inbuilt facility.

## KNITTING INSTRUCTIONS

### Double jacquard

1 Cast on in FNR with MY over 35/35 needles on each bed. Knit 4 circular rows at TD 2/2 and 1 or 2 rows plain rib. COL.

2 Insert punchcard, lock on row 1. Knit 1 row. COR.

3 Release card, set machine to slip, knit 1 row. The pattern needles are selected. COL.

4 Change to CY. Knit 2 rows. The background needles are selected.

5 Change to MY. Knit 2 rows.

Continue in this way until two complete patterns have been worked.

6 Transfer all the stitches to the main bed. Knit 1 row at TD10. Cast off. Pull the fabric to shape widthways and lengthways. Steam press the fabric immediately as this is only a test piece.

If the sample piece was knitted without problems and you like the texture, I suggest you knit a tension piece in preparation for your first garment. An actual tension piece is best left to rest overnight before steam pressing to allow the yarn to relax.

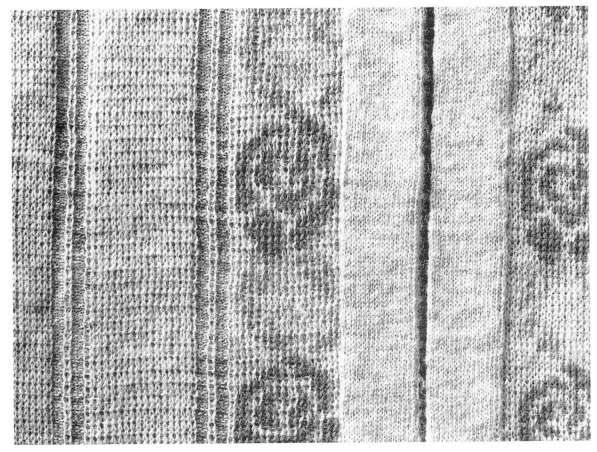

*64 Embossed jacquard*

## EMBOSSED JACQUARD

Embossed jacquard is double jacquard knitted in panels with sections of the ribber fabric exposed where the main bed needles have been taken out of work (*Fig. 64*). It is preferable to use striper jacquard to produce a soft fabric. Bird's-eye jacquard can be used if you prefer – this would produce a slightly more dense fabric with speckled sections instead of striped sections between the pattern panels.

In the previous chapter we used long stitch, which is a version of double jacquard without the patterning, to knit in panels. This time the panels will have two colours in every row. It is possible to use the same width panels as in the long stitch skirt but the pattern would have to be very small. Any Fair Isle punchcard which has sections which are not punched for the whole length of the punchcard can be used for embossed jacquard. The punchcard in Fig. 63a is ideal.

The unpunched sections indicate the stitches which need to be transferred to the ribber bed. Knit a test piece using the punchcard in Fig. 63 to see just where the pattern sections are placed on the needlebed. If your selection is incorrect, part of the patterning may have vanished into the empty needle section!

*1  Tam-o'-shanters and gloves*

2 *Autumn scene scarf*

*3 Left: Petal slip stitch jacket*

*4 Below: Butterfly slip stitch (detail)*

5 Left: Poppy slipover

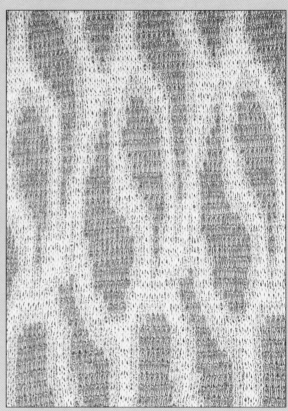

6 Three colours in a row (detail above: knitside and purlside)

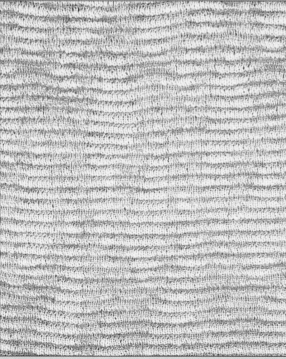

7 Right: Double jacquard coat (courtesy Bradford Museums)

8 Left: Embossed jacquard pleat with corded edge (detail)

9 Right: Tuck and slip mosaic slipover

*10 Right: Multicoloured dress*

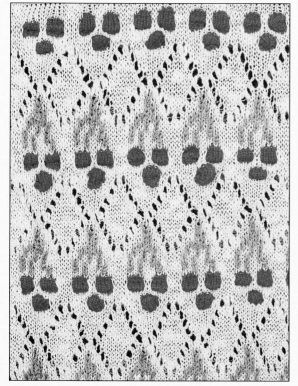

*11 Left: Cherries, Fair Isle and lace*

12  *Ridge pleat skirt*

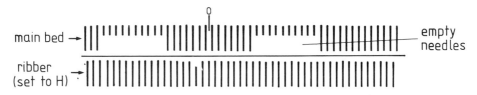

main bed → | empty needles

ribber (set to H) →

*65 Needle arrangement for embossed jacquard*

## KNITTING INSTRUCTIONS

### Embossed jacquard

1 Cast on in FNR as for ordinary double jacquard.

2 Select for the first row of pattern. Transfer the needles on the unpunched section of the card to the ribber (*Fig. 65*) and continue knitting as you

would for ordinary double jacquard, changing colour every two rows as before. Stripes will appear where the stitches were transferred and the panels will have the leaf and flower design.

All-over patterns in embossed jacquard are simple to knit but, with patterning on the knit panels and stripes on the purl panels, the design may look too

*66 Jacket in embossed jacquard*

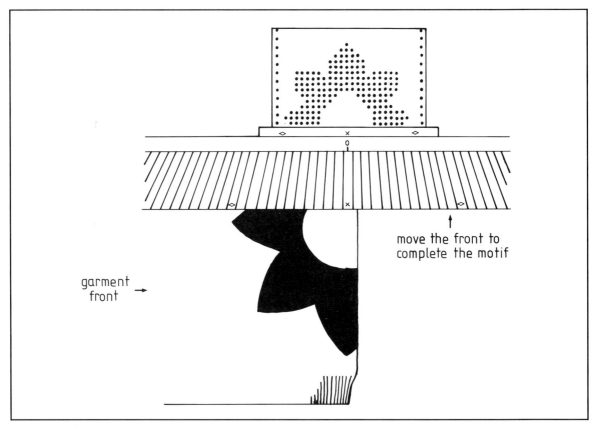

67  *Centring a front*

fussy. The Brother punchcard is a vertical pattern and looks quite acceptable. The rose pattern (*Fig. 62*) looks beautiful as a border around the bottom of a jacket, continuing as a single motif down the front at each side of the front bands (*Fig. 66*).

On punchcard machines single-motif knitting in embossed jacquard is quite tedious to do but very rewarding. Full details are given in the colour changer manuals. The method entails selecting the background needles by hand to keep the pattern correct.

The pattern panels outline the jacket. On the front, where the single motifs are worked, blocks of different colours are formed giving a checked appearance to the main body of the jacket.

To give a professional look to the garment the same colour-change sequence must be used on the back and the sleeves. Fortunately the fronts are the

only parts which require a single-motif setting. Knit the back and sleeves first so that you become familiar with the colour-change sequence. The fronts are best knitted either side of 0 but in this case because the punchcard centre is the centre of the needlebed it is necessary to shift the pattern a few stitches to the left or right to ensure a complete single motif on each front (*Fig. 67*).

Additional interest can be added by leaving the two centre stitches of the purl panels in work on the main bed.

## VARIATIONS

The fabric produced by embossed double jacquard is in two thicknesses: the pattern panels are double thickness, the exposed sections are single thickness.

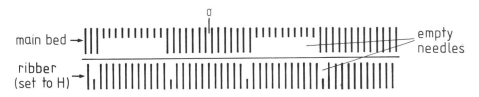

68 *Embossed jacquard pleat arrangement*

This difference raises the pattern panels above the striped sections, forming a mock pleat. If a needle is taken out of work on the ribber at each side of the pattern panels a more definite pleat is formed.

The punchcard in Fig. 63 is designed so that it only uses ten needles for the pattern panels leaving fourteen stitches available for use on the ribber. As the pattern looks better with an outline, two stitches each side of the pattern were used for this purpose and the remaining ten stitches were transferred to the ribber bed (*Fig. 65*).

1 To highlight the different fabric thicknesses, one needle each side of the pattern panel was transferred from the ribber bed to the main bed (*Fig. 68*). The result is quite striking. The dark solid panels with the vertical pattern stand proud of the horizontal multicoloured stripes to form a mock pleat.

2 To further emphasize the pleats and reduce the bulk at the hip, remove two more stitches from the ribber section next to the ones already empty (*Fig. 69*).

69 *Embossed jacquard pleat (variation 2): needle arrangement (top)
and pleat with two needles out of work (bottom)*

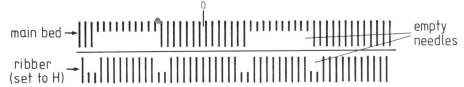

## Brother Special

What would happen if the bird's-eye setting was used to produce a speckled backing? In theory the stripes should break up and the colours should merge. In fact all that results is a muddle. The $1 \times 1$ setting must have an even number of stitches on the needlebed for the bird's-eye backing.

At first I could not understand what had happened and, whilst investigating, I inadvertently set the carriage to KCI. Because of the empty needles, the first and last needle of each pattern panel was selected to knit. Each pleat had an edging which knitted every row, producing a corded finish in the contrast colours (*colour plate 8*).

*Note* Punchcard machines from the 860 upwards can use this method by leaving the end needle cams in operation.

*70 Lined jacquard: a Original design  b Adapted punchcard*

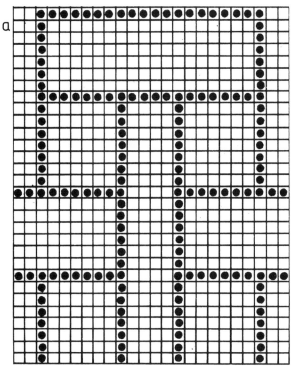

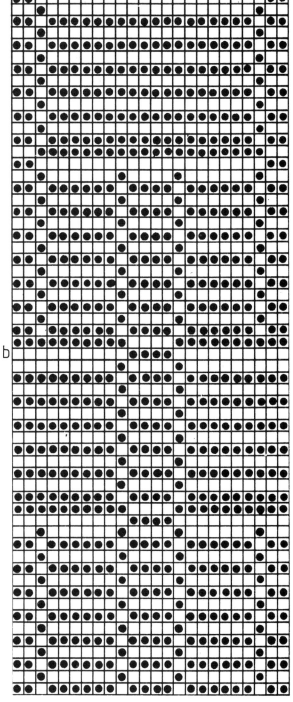

# LINED JACQUARD

Lined jacquard is a form of double-bed knitting not unlike double jacquard except that the fabric is knitted on each bed independently. At intervals along the row, selected stitches are knitted on both beds to connect the two fabrics.

If the fabric is knitted in two colours then the face side of the knitting has two colours and the backing is in the contrast colour. To obtain this separation, special cards need to be punched to isolate each colour (*Fig. 70a and 70b*).

### Designing lined and quilted jacquard cards

1 Two rows on the punchcard are required for each row of the pattern. Mark the new card in two-row sections and mark each section with the appropriate row number.

2 The blank spaces of the design are marked on the first row of the sequence.

3 The marked sections of the design are marked on the second row of the sequence.

## Knitting details for lined and quilted jacquard

1 The main carriage is set to slip and elongation throughout the knitting. The Knitmaster 500 and 560 must have the sheet double marked. Each two-row sequence must be identical, unlike the double jacquard fabric where each row in a sequence may be different.

2 The ribber setting is changed to slip every two rows. When only a small number of needles are selected on the main bed, the ribber cam needs to be set to knit. When large numbers of needles are selected on the main bed then the ribber must slip.

Altering the ribber setting every two rows is not as tedious as it may seem. Like anything with a regular sequence, the changeover becomes automatic.

### Knitmaster special

The Knitmaster SRP 60N ribber changes the cam setting automatically which speeds up the work. The ribber carriage must be taken to the extreme left of the needlebed for the autoset lever to trip the driving cam (*Fig. 60*).

The tension has to be balanced as the fabric needs to be flat (try 5/4). The sections knitted in main yarn have a more intense colour than in double jacquard as the colour is not broken up by the contrast yarn.

It is possible to knit a fabric in lined jacquard using different yarn thicknesses. The basic hexagon used in quilting looks fascinating if invisible yarn is used in one feeder. In Fig. 71 some pockets which formed were filled with flower-shaped beads to create an illusion of floating flowers. The invisible yarn is 100% nylon and produces a very hard feel to the fabric. If, however, you wish to cause a stir when you go out, then this is the way to do it!

The cards for lined jacquard can have intricate patterns as the pockets are not usually filled. This method of knitting is an ideal way of producing float-free fabric with good colour definition. Fine yarns are essential to produce a soft fluid fabric but if a blanket is to be knitted, a thicker yarn up to 3-ply can be used as there are only a few stitches which knit on both beds at the same time.

# QUILTED JACQUARD

Quilted jacquard is similar to lined jacquard. The cards have the same marking and it is knitted in exactly the same way. The only difference between them is that the TD on the main bed is turned up as high as possible without the stitches lifting off the needles to form a loose front to the pocket (try TD 9/3).

As the knitting progresses, a thin wadding is added between the two beds before each pocket is closed by the punchcard. The fabric can be knitted without inserting the wadding, to produce a smooth-backed fabric with a crumpled face side. Each of the finishes is attractive (*Fig. 72*).

101

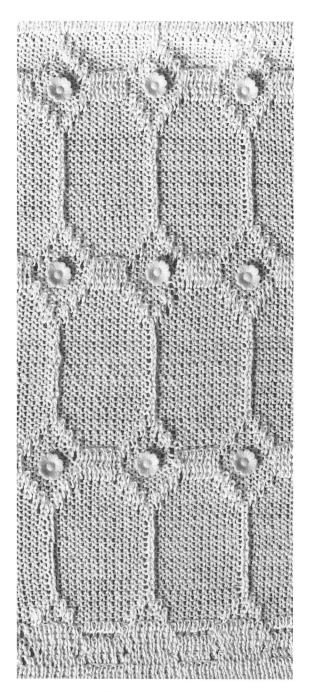 

71 *Lined jacquard with invisible thread*

72  Lined jacquard (left) and quilted jacquard (right)

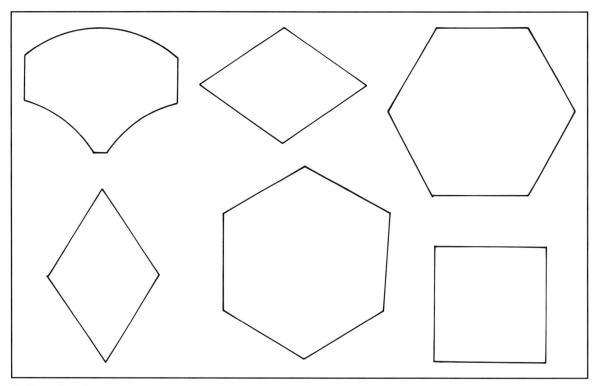

73 *Shapes for quilting*

There are lots of traditional shapes for patchwork (*Fig. 73*) which can be converted to punchcards and used for quilting. Three of the shapes in Fig. 73 – the clamshell, a small octagon and the wide diamond – are reproduced in Fig. 74 with the correct marking. More examples are included in *The Machine Knitter's Book of the Ribber*, Volume 2, by Kathleen Kinder.

It is difficult to fill an odd-shaped pocket whilst it is still on the machine. Knit a sample of the quilting. Measure the size and shape of the pocket and cut out a few pieces of foam to fit. When the widest part of the shape has been knitted, lower the ribber slightly and place the cutout shapes into the pocket which has formed. Take care that the foam does not catch in the needles for the next few rows.

74 *Patterns for quilting* (opposite)

## BLISTER JACQUARD

Blister stitch is an extension of lined and quilted jacquard. The sections which are separated from the backing form blisters consisting of extra stocking stitch rows, either in the same colour as the backing or in a completely different colour, depending on the method used.

To produce a raised double-bed fabric it is necessary to knit more rows on one bed than on the other. In Chapter 6 the double-bed pintucks are an example of this type of texturing. The pintucks show that the Japanese machines are able to cope with extra rows being knitted on one or other of the needlebeds but pintucks are only the beginning of the story. They are non-selective in that all the stitches on the needlebed that are set to knit, will knit.

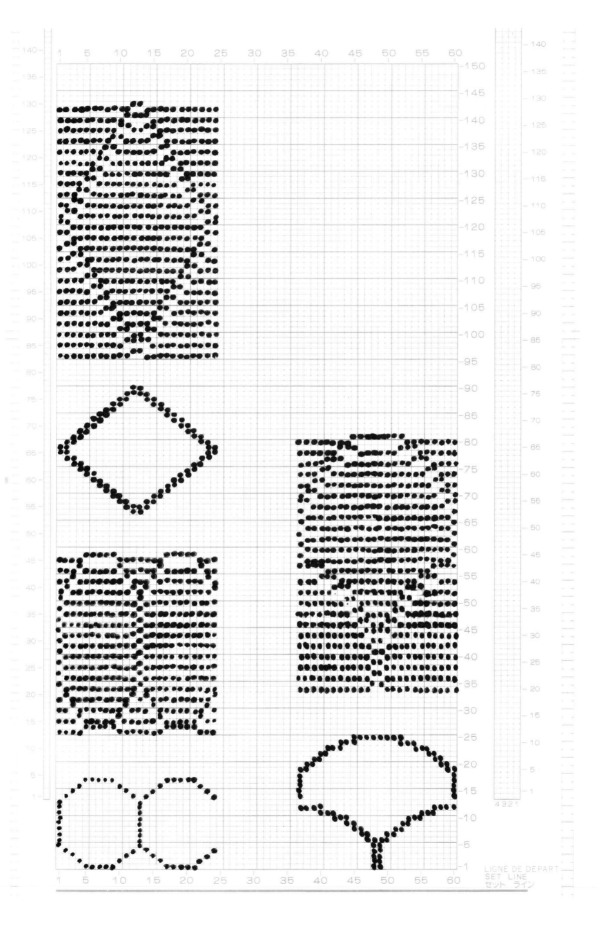

75 *Blister stitch*

Blister stitch produces patches of knitting which are separate from the ribber fabric in pattern areas and are joined in the background areas. The introduction of cards specially designed for quilted and lined jacquard led to the development of the technique which can be used to produce quite intricate blister patterns (*Fig. 75*).

As seen in the previous chapter the different settings used on the ribber can alter the appearance of the fabric. In Chapter 6, when knitting three colours in a row on the double bed, the ribber is set to slip one way to reduce the number of backing rows by half. The same principle is used for blister stitch to increase the number of rows knitted in certain sections, on the knit side of the fabric. This indicated a way of further reducing the number of rows knitted on the ribber without having to interfere with the punchcard sequence.

Blister stitch requires even more rows to be knitted on one bed than the other. Until now it was thought that the only way to increase the number of rows was to stop the punchcard and knit the extra rows before releasing the card, allowing it to rotate and pick up the pattern until the next blister section is reached.

When knitting quilted and lined jacquard in two colours the ribber setting needs to be altered after every two-row sequence. The ribber is set to knit with the main (background) yarn for two rows. The two-row sequence in contrast (pattern) yarn is knitted with the ribber set to slip both ways. This means that the main bed knits twice as many rows as the ribber. To increase the number of rows on the main bed without having to repunch the card is quite easy. Simply set the left cam on the ribber and leave it up throughout the knitting. With a card punched as for quilted and lined jacquard and the machine set to elongation, the sequence is as follows:

2 rows BY: main bed slip. Ribber bed L button slip, R button normal.

2 rows CY: main bed slip. Ribber bed slip both ways.

Thus one backing row is knitted to four rows of knitting on the main bed. There are still only two rows in the blister but the extra backing row, which is released by the ribber cam change, helps to produce a more pronounced blister. To further increase the size of the blister, use a tension of approximately 6/3.

When knitting the contrast colour rows with the ribber set to slip you are knitting on the main bed only. This means that there are floats across the knitting from one blister to another just as there are in single-bed Fair Isle. They will be enclosed in the fabric when the next background sequence is knitted.

Although it cannot be classed as automatic, because of the ribber alterations, the method does produce a pronounced blister in the fabric without any alterations to the punchcard movement.

With this type of knitting the raised (contrast colour) areas have a stronger colour than in double jacquard. The flat areas have a mix of both but the contrast yarn is stranded across inside the fabric, not knitted in as in double jacquard.

### Brother 910 Special

Using the above method on this machine there is no need to redraw designs. The 910 can combine the double jacquard setting, elongation and the colour change, so any Fair Isle card can be used. It is better to use designs which are not too complicated. Experiment – you may be pleasantly surprised.

## Knitmaster 500 and 560

Knitmaster electronic machine users will have to double mark the mylar sheet. Then proceed as for the Brother electronic machines.

The balance of tension between the two needlebeds and the choice of yarn can make or mar the success of this type of stitch. When knitting lined jacquard the tensions are balanced so that the fabric lies flat. Quilted jacquard, however, needs the main bed tension to be turned up as high as the yarn will take without the stitches lifting off the needle and to allow room for the pocket to be stuffed with wadding or foam.

These two types of knitting require slightly different punchcards. Quilted jacquard must have simple outlines to allow for the filling of the pockets and to give definition to the stuffed shape. Lined jacquard can have designs which are more complicated because the pockets will not be filled. Blister

*76 Sunset scene*

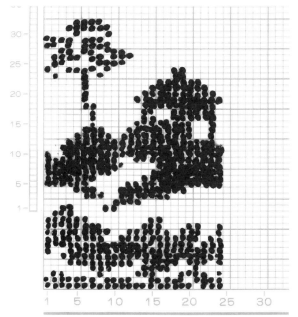

stitch falls into this category. The pockets can be filled if you wish but the blisters are interesting enough without being emphasized.

There are more rows to be knitted on the main bed than on the ribber and if the main bed tension is too high the stitches lift off the needles causing dropped stitches. Aim to have the tension on the main bed as high as possible to form loose folds of fabric on the surface of the knitting. You will know whether you have got it right if the knitting goes smoothly without stitches lifting from the needles. There is certainly no substitute for practising and testing.

Once these problems are solved it is easy to spot suitable cards for this treatment. An old punchcard (*Fig. 76*), designed when picture knitting was all the rage, seemed to have possibilities. Punch the card as given for quilted and lined jacquard. As before the main bed is set to elongation but the ribber is set for blister stitch.

Do not forget that with any design you can select the section you wish to emphasize with blisters. It is better to knit the larger sections as a blister with just a few stitches in between used to connect the two fabrics. The long floats formed in the fabric by the small areas of blister are best dealt with immediately they are formed; otherwise they may be caught in the ribber needles when the next background row which connects the two fabrics is knitted.

One solution is to push one or two needles to upper working position on the ribber bed for a few rows. The selected needles must be in the centre of the background area. They will knit in the colour of the blisters. The extra pull these stitches cause on the floats helps them to stay in place ready for the next two rows of knitting.

The textured fabrics produced in Chapters 6 and 7 illustrate just how far we have progressed from the time when, apart from plain ribs, double jacquard was the only other use for a ribber. As our confidence grows so does our realization of their hidden potential. A ribber does not double but trebles the types of fabric which the machine can produce. We have to thank Mary Weaver, Kathleen Kinder and many other people for encouraging us to investigate double-bed fabrics. How much further is there to go?

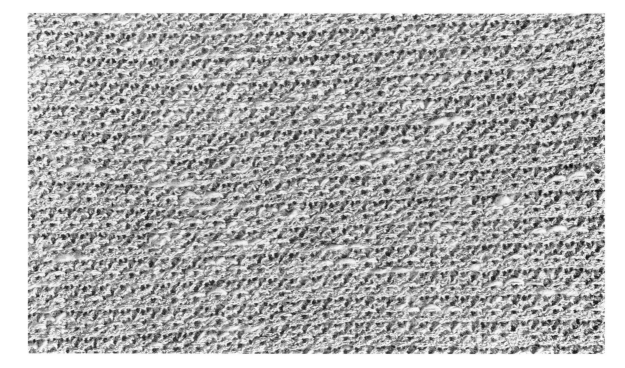

# 8 Slip and mix

In previous chapters we have explored the various applications of the slip setting. Each aspect of the stitch has been studied in isolation. By concentrating on the many different ways slip stitch can be used we have learned what a versatile stitch it is for patterning on either the single- or double-bed machine. With the knowledge we have gained it is time to combine slip stitch with tuck, Fair Isle and lace to see how they react with the new-style slip stitch which has been developed.

Some stitch combinations are possible on one type of machine and are totally impractical on another. Where possible alternatives are included. Some of the stitch combinations which can be used together with the slip setting are as follows:

1 Tuck and slip

2 Fair Isle and slip

3 Lace and slip

4 Punch lace and slip

5 Fair Isle, lace and slip

## PATTERN NOTES

1 Only categories 1 and 5 are true combination fabrics as the carriage is knitting each setting selectively over the whole of every row.

2 In categories 2, 3 and 4 the fabric is produced by knitting a few rows with one setting then a few rows

*77 Tuck and slip: knit side (top) and purl side (bottom)*

with the other. The way these stitch combinations interact gives the illusion that they are knitted in one row instead of separately.

## TUCK AND SLIP

In the Introduction we noted the similarities between tuck and slip and also the differences. The similarities make the two settings an obvious first choice for a combination fabric. The differences – tuck widens a fabric and slip narrows it – would seem to suggest that they are not compatible. If the stitches are mixed, however, interesting fabrics can be produced (*Fig. 77*). There are different ways of combining the two settings.

1 Knit 1 row tuck, 1 row slip.

2 Knit 1 row slip, 1 row tuck.

3 Knit a few rows tuck then a few rows slip.

4 Knit a few rows slip then a few rows tuck.

The first two settings are automatic on the Brother which simplifies the knitting.

On the Knitmaster it is only necessary to move the lever one place around the dial and back again, which is simple enough.

The Passap requires two movements to change the cam setting. In this case, only attempt combinations of three or four rows of each setting so that there are not as many cam changes.

*Punchcard pattern sheet 7*

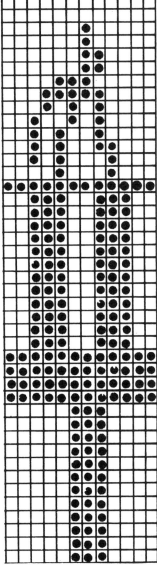

38

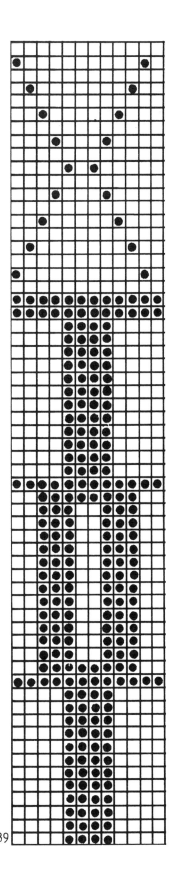

39

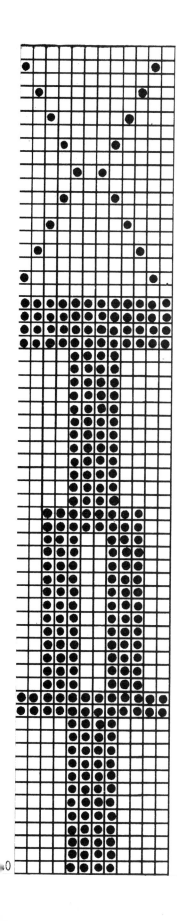

41

42

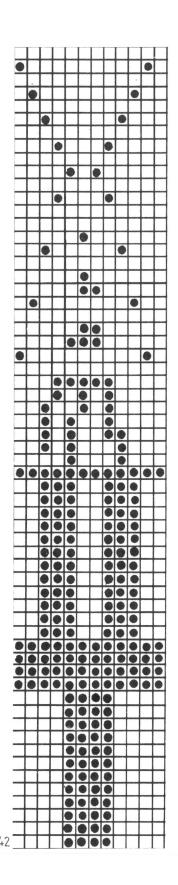

There are, as we know, many similarities between tuck and slip but a closer look at the different way each cam setting places its floats on the fabric will help when designing with specific effects in mind.

Slip stitch has floats across the unselected needles. These floats lie on the surface of the fabric and tend to rest at the bottom of the stitch when the fabric is relaxed (*Fig. 1b*).

Tuck stitch holds loops of yarn in the needle head for the required number of rows. These loops are then knitted in. When the fabric is relaxed the loops are held by the background yarn at the top of the stitch (*Fig. 1a*).

The use of a combination of the two stitches produces totally different results depending on which stitch is knitted first.

### Brother

1 Tuck and slip: right tuck button and left part button in.

2 Slip and tuck: left tuck button and right part button in.

There are so many variations possible with this setting that it would take a book to cover them all. While working on this I remembered a fabric I had seen a long time ago. The fabric was in the form of pleats which used a combination of slip and tuck together with thick and thin yarn.

The yarns I selected for the experiments, a 2/30s cotton and two ends of Texere 4-ply crepe, were a perfect foil for each other. Any crisp crepe yarn will do but make sure it is soft enough not to strain the machine.

At the beginning of this section I explained the way tuck and slip place their pattern loops on the fabric. By using this knowledge it is possible to decide the shape of the design in the stripe.

To emphasize the difference in the yarn thicknesses I have inserted two rows of stocking stitch between each two-row pattern rows. The stocking stitch rows are always knitted in fine yarn. The patterning rows are always knitted in the two ends of 4-ply.

As the yarn is to be changed every two rows the colour changer is used. This means that the patterning begins on the left. The five punchcards I used are adaptations of basic cards which have been punched out in full rather than using the elongation button (*Fig. 78a–e*).

*Note* Passap owners: if you decide to punch a card, punch it singly as the Deco will double the rows automatically when set to 2.

*78 Punchcards for tuck and slip*

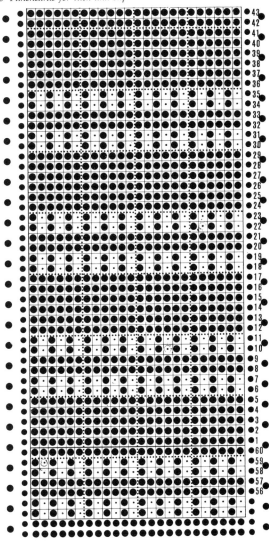

When the left tuck button and the right part button are both depressed and the row is knitted from the left to the right, the first row will slip. This means that the floats which form across the non-selected needles will rest at the bottom of the knitted stitches. When knitting the next row, which will tuck, the loops, formed by the non-selected needles, will be held at the top of the knitted stitches.

Depending on which punchcard you use, i.e. whether the punched holes are alternated (*Fig. 78b*) or

are in line (*Fig. 78a*) with each other, you will have stripes with either alternating loops, which look like giant chain stitches, or overlapping loops which suggest a lazy-daisy-stitch stripe (*Fig. 79*).

This is because of the use of two extremes in yarn thickness. The tension dial, approximately 6, remains the same throughout the knitting. When the fabric is released from the machine the fine yarn contracts to its natural size, which pulls in the thick yarn, allowing it to form interesting effects on the fabric.

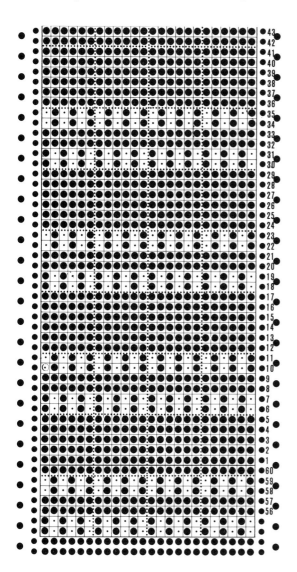

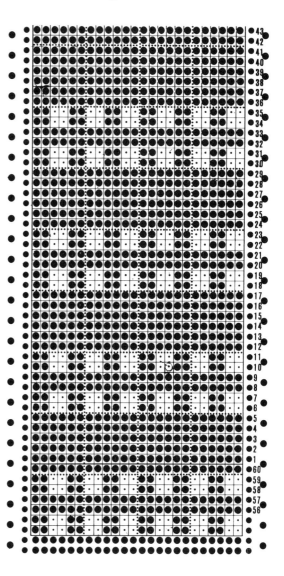

The crisp sheen of the crepe was emphasized by its being used double on a background of fine yarn. This fabric is the nearest I have come to knitting a form of guipure lace. There are drawbacks as the slip-stitch floats are quite loose and liable to catch when worn. The samples were knitted in white and would make a beautiful bridal fabric. So far the patterns are in stripes and I have not worked out how to reproduce the effect in an all-over fabric.

Try the following sequences with each of the five punchcards. You will be surprised and delighted with the results.

## Tuck and slip combinations for use with special punchcards

Always begin at the left if using a colour changer.

*78 Punchcards continued*

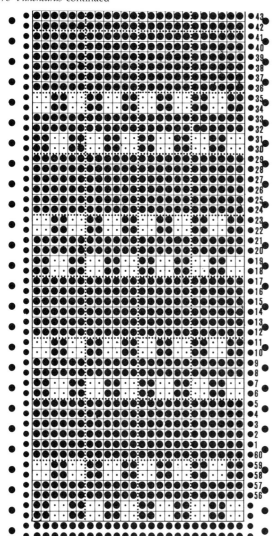

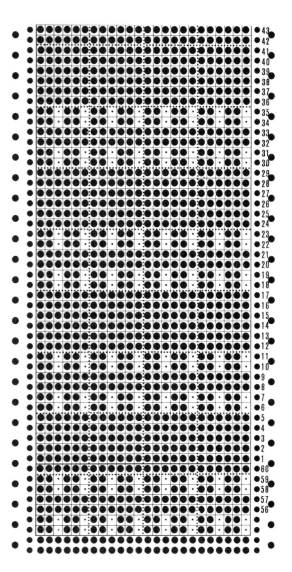

114

## SEQUENCE 1

Row 1  Tuck in thick yarn.

Row 2  Slip in thick yarn.

Rows 3 and 4  Stocking stitch in thin yarn.

Work the above sequence then rows 1 and 2 once more. RC6.

Knit 6 rows stocking stitch in thin yarn. RC12.

## SEQUENCE 2

Row 1  Slip in thick yarn.

Row 2  Tuck in thick yarn.

Rows 3 and 4  Stocking stitch in thin yarn.

Work the above 4-row sequence then rows 1 and 2 once more. RC6.

Knit 6 rows stocking stitch in thin yarn. RC12.

*79 Tuck and slip in thick and thin yarns*

## SEQUENCE 3

Rows 1 and 2  Tuck in thick yarn.

Rows 3 and 4  Stocking stitch in thin yarn.

Rows 5 and 6  Slip in thick yarn.

Rows 7–12  Stocking stitch in thin yarn.

## SEQUENCE 4

Rows 1 and 2  Slip in thick yarn.

Rows 3 and 4  Stocking stitch in thin yarn.

Rows 5 and 6  Tuck in thick yarn.

Rows 7–12  Stocking stitch in thin yarn.

There are many more combinations of punchcards and patterns. Experiment and find out some of your own. Remember to write down how each was done. It can be difficult to reproduce an effect if you are unable to recall how the carriage was set or which yarn-change sequence you used.

Still following the principle of using one row slip, one row tuck and changing colour every two rows, I returned to the mosaics described in Chapter 3. The yarns I used were of different textures but similar thickness. The effect was quite stunning. The fabric was the thickness of a 4-ply stocking stitch with the occasional float over two stitches. The knit side of the fabric had raised nodules which when knitted in a shiny yarn caught the light in a most attractive way (*colour plate 9*).

# FAIR ISLE AND SLIP

The combination of Fair Isle with slip developed after I had designed the cherries. There was a need to provide stems for the cherries to produce a realistic bunch of fruit. Fair Isle was the obvious choice. Each setting is knitted separately but the patterns merge very well because of the distortion caused by the

115

many rows of slip stitch. To eliminate large floats the card is based on 12 stitches instead of 24. Floats have been virtually eliminated in the slip section of the design. Unfortunately Fair Isle always produces strands of yarn across the back of the work.

The design is fairly easy to knit. The only cam change is from slip to Fair Isle and as this occurs when the contrast yarn has to be threaded in, it should be easy to remember.

## KNITTING INSTRUCTIONS

### Fair Isle and Slip (*PP38*)

> *Yarn A* background yarn: two strands Hobby (white or black)
>
> *Yarn B* cherries: acrylic crepe (red)
>
> *Yarn C* stems: bouclé and cotton mix (green)

### Brother electronic machines

Programme the machine as an all-over pattern (pattern selector B).

### Knitmaster 500 and 560

NIC in centre position. PC at edge of knitting. Pattern widther to 12.

### Punchcard machines

> Set up as for pattern knitting.
>
> Thread up single-bed colour changer.
>
> Cast on over 40/40 stitches in WY and knit a few rows. COL.
>
> Change to yarn A and knit 1 row to the right. COR.
>
> Set machine to memorize the pattern. Knit 1 row from right to left.
>
> Set carriage to slip.
>
> 1 Change to yarn B. RC000. Knit to RC12. stop. Before knitting this row take a latch tool upwards behind the long floats and pull the last

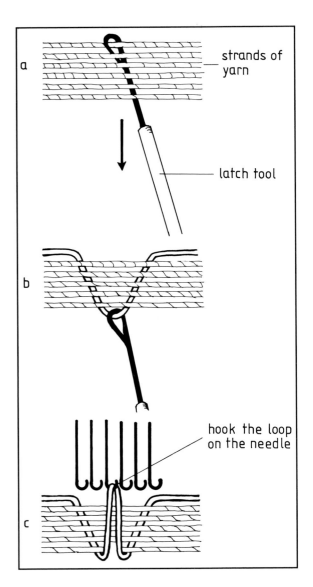

*80 Collecting the floats*

row knitted in yarn B gently down behind the remaining floats. Lift the hooked loop onto one of the non-selected needles thus enclosing them in a strand of yarn (*Fig. 80*).

2 Change to yarn A. Knit 4 rows. RC16.

3 Change to yarn B. Knit to RC28.

4 Change to yarn A. Knit 1 row to the right. This row selects the Fair Isle pattern. Thread yarn C into the Fair Isle feeder, change the cam lever to Fair Isle and knit to the end of the pattern.

## LACE AND SLIP

### (Brother Special)

In my childhood the ritual of new clothes at Whitsuntide was preceded by months of work by my mother who embroidered and smocked matching dresses for my sister and me. In addition, our socks, in a beautiful lace pattern, and our cardigans were hand knitted. One cardigan in particular was brought to mind when looking through some old knitting patterns. The Tyrolean-style cardigan had bobbles arranged in a diamond shape, in the centre of which was an embroidered flower. The discovery, described in Chapter 3, that small flowers could be knitted inspired me to attempt a similar type of pattern with flowers in the centre of a lace diamond.

Any of the flower braid patterns with a 12-stitch base can be used for the all-over fabric. PP21 was the most effective. The design was altered to reduce the amount of green in the centre (*colour plate 10*).

The lace pattern I selected is an extremely simple one with only one blank row between each lace selection. The lace pattern is arranged to slot into the space between the flowers.

### KNITTING INSTRUCTIONS

#### Lace and slip (PP38)

#### Brother 910 and 950

Insert the programme, remembering to include one extra row at the end of the pattern. Follow the instructions for Fair Isle and slip to the end of step 3. All the needles are selected.

4 Change to yarn A. Knit 1 row to the right. All needles are in normal WP. Release KCII, knit 1 row to the left.

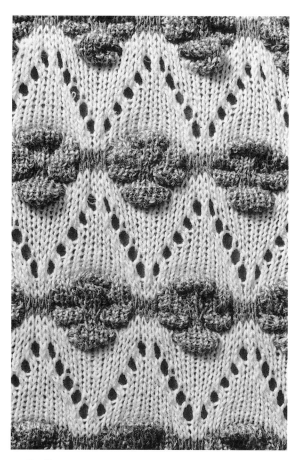

81 *Small pansy*

5 Place the lace carriage on the *right* of the machine and take it across the needlebed to the left and back again.

6 Continue with the lace only until the card returns to row 1.

Repeat the above steps.

The shape of the small flower seemed to be a little out of balance and I decided to add another stitch to each petal on the centre row of the flower to widen it slightly. In so doing I lost my concentration and forgot to change colour on the two stocking stitch rows after the first row of petals. The result was another breakthrough (*Fig. 81*).

117

Yet again an alteration to the colour-change sequence has produced an entirely different look to a design. Here we are with a simplified and smaller pansy shape which will fit into the 12-stitch discipline in which we are working. The card was altered slightly to eliminate two of the stocking stitch rows between the flowers (*PP39*).

We now have two different styles of flowers to place in between the lace sections. As they both have the same-width pattern card each flower shape can be knitted on its own in a design or they can be alternated, just as you wish.

The way the pattern is designed it is not possible to have different colours dotted around the fabric unless you use the flower braid outlined in Chapter 5 and use it as an insert. The flowers have to be in stripes of one colour. I like to have green mixed in with the flower colour but not many flowers have green centres. If you find you cannot live with this, knit in a bead of the required colour. Each row of flowers could be a different colour. Wind off small balls of the colours you have selected and as one row of flowers is complete, break off the yarn behind the machine and join in a fresh colour with a knot. Pull the yarn through the yarn mast until the knot passes through the colour changer. Hook it on the yarn clip until you are ready to use it. This way there is no need to re-thread the machine.

The stock of yarn you have built up over the years will come in useful. Think of all the cone ends of yarn you have on the shelf and how effective they will look knitted up into flowers.

## PUNCH LACE AND SLIP

To produce a fabric combination of slip and lace on the Knitmaster machines the carriages have to be changed when alternating between slip and lace. To simplify this, punch lace can be used instead of transfer lace with equal success. The punch lace is not as noticeable as the ordinary lace but it is quite acceptable as an alternative.

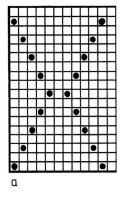
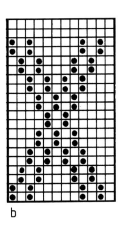

*82 Converting transfer lace to punch lace: a Transfer lace b Punch lace*

The yarn is changed quite often which means that the colour changer needs to be used. This is quite useful as the thread for the lace can be held in the yarn holder together with the other colours needed to knit the pattern. When the lace section is ready to be knitted it is a simple matter to thread the fine yarn into the second feeder, change the cam lever to punch lace and knit until the card returns to the beginning of the pattern.

The punch lace pattern is adapted from the lace card used in the previous section. The lace had only one blank row between each row of lace marks. These blank rows were used to form the double height markings normal for punch lace (*Fig. 82*).

The slip section of the card is identical to that for the other machines. I found that on the 560 it is preferable to leave the Russell levers set as for punch lace to ensure that the first needle will knit, and hold the stitch, when it is pushed to holding position at the beginning of each row. If the needles are pushed to holding position at each end of every row the left-hand stitch has a tendency to drop.

The mylar sheet was marked with double marking on all the machine types as there are slight alterations to the punchcard which only occur on one row. These flowers, then, cannot be knitted exactly the same on the Passap unless the pushers are altered manually.

## KNITTING INSTRUCTIONS

### Punch lace and slip (*PP41*)

*Yarn*

*Colour 1* background

*Colour 2* flower

*Colour 3* green

*Colour 4* fine yarn

Set the machine for normal pattern knitting. Select the first row of the punch lace and take the memory. COL.

1 Using colour 1 in feeder 1 and the lace yarn in feeder 2. Set the machine for punch lace, knit until the card returns to row 1.

2 Change the cam lever to slip. Change the yarn and knit 12 rows in colour 2. STOP. Take the latch tool up behind the long floats and pull the last row knitted, in colour 2, gently down behind the remaining floats. Lift the hooked loop onto one of the needles thus enclosing them in a strand of yarn (*see Fig. 80*).

3 Knit 2 rows in colour 3.

4 Knit 12 rows in colour 2.

5 Knit 2 rows in colour 3.

6 Knit 12 rows in colour 2. STOP. Repeat the yarn wrap in step 2.

7 Change the cam lever to punchlace, thread up the machine and continue until the card returns to row 1.

Repeat steps 2–7 for the required number of rows.

As with transfer lace the punch lace slots into the distortion in the fabric, formed by the slip sections, giving the impression that the two settings have been knitted together instead of separately (Fig. 83).

The wrapping of the floats in step 2 helps to tidy the fabric and to stabilize it. The way the floats are wrapped together helps to create more distortion in the fabric by pulling the flowers into shape and

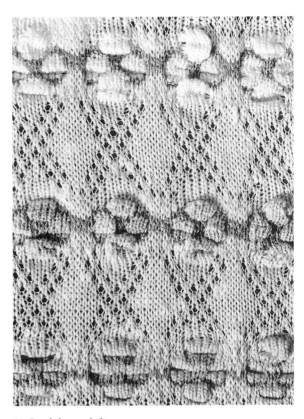

83 *Punch lace and slip*

keeping them there. The collection of the floats into a roll effectively stops them spreading into the lace sections where they would be visible and allows them to hide behind the two rows of stocking stitch knitted in colour 3 in the middle of the flower pattern.

# FAIR ISLE, SLIP AND LACE

## (Brother Special)

There are four quite distinct pattern sections, each with its own characteristic which produces a different-width fabric. The varying width of fabric produced by each setting is not noticeable when a complete garment is made.

119

Tension pieces can be knitted and measured as usual, or use the motif method (*Chapter 1, Tension guide* and *Chapter 10, Petal slip stitch jacket*). If the motif method is used, complete patterns are being worked and the different fabrics will combine to form a completely new textile with its own characteristics.

## Brother 910 and 950 (*PP42*)

Programme the machine as an all-over pattern, remembering to include one extra blank row at the end of the design.

### Punchcard machines
Use the punchcard in Fig. 84.

### KNITTING INSTRUCTIONS

Follow the instructions for Fair Isle and slip to the end of step 3. All the needles are selected.

4 Change to yarn A. Knit 1 row to the right. The needles for Fair Isle are selected. Thread yarn C into the Fair Isle feeder. Set the machine to Fair Isle and knit 7 rows. COL.

5 Place the lace carriage on the *right* of the machine and take it across the needlebed to the left and back again. The first row of lace has been worked and the needles are selected for Fair Isle.

*Note* Punchcard machines: When the lace carriage is moved from right to left the lace needles are selected. They are empty and will be placed in their correct position when the lace carriage is returned to the right. When the Fair Isle and lace have been worked the lace selection returns to normal.

Continue in this way until no needles are selected when knitting with the main carriage. COR. Break off yarn C, release the Fair Isle button and knit to the left. Release KC.

6 Continue with the lace only until the card returns to row 1.

Repeat the above steps.

The fabric produced by this punchcard is a step forward for machine knitters which could be developed further. The lace was pulled up into the area of the cherries making it look as if it was knitted on the same row (*Fig. 85* and *colour plate 11*).

*84  Fair Isle, lace and slip*

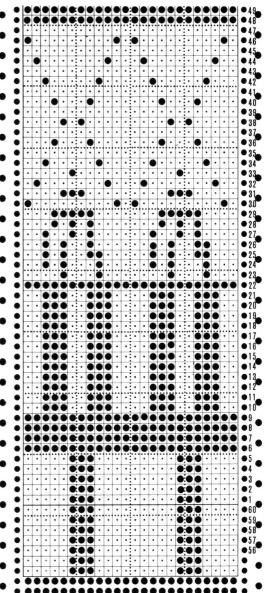

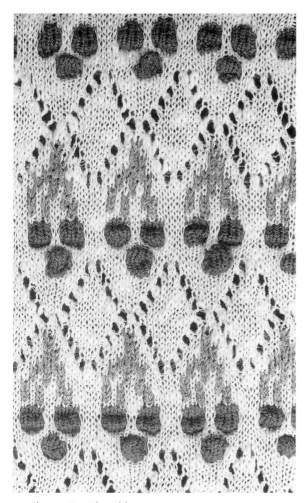

85 *Cherries, Fair Isle and lace*

The development of the cherries from petal slip stitch was quite exciting. As soon as I realized how best to deal with the long floats, other ideas began to emerge. Using the same principle it should be possible to knit quite realistic bunches of grapes onto a garment if you wish!

Yarn texture and colour are most important. The original Tyrolean designs have a white or cream wool background with flowers of different colours dotted about the pattern. For these samples I used an undyed cotton, approximately 2-ply thickness, for the background. The Fair Isle yarn was a mixture of cotton and bouclé which was slightly thicker. The flowers and the cherries were knitted in the 4-ply acrylic crepe mentioned previously. These three yarns gave me an excellent mix of textures. The shine of the acrylic, the roughness of the stems and leaves and the matt neutral background combine very well. The thickness of the yarn does not matter too much as long as the fabric is not too heavy.

Occasionally the yarn you select, even though it is the same type, will knit up differently as the colour is changed. The yarn absorbs the dye at varying rates depending on the moisture content in the fibre when the yarn is being dyed. This affects the thickness of the yarn and alters the size of the flowers. With this type of slip stitch the tension needs to be one whole number higher than would normally be expected, to compensate for the pull in of the fabric. As long as the tension you have selected is able to cope with yarn which varies slightly in thickness, all will be well.

The correct 'dressing' of the fabric after it is released from the machine is vital. After knitting so many samples I can tell whether a design is a success or not without any treatment at all. In the beginning it was disappointing as I was unable to see the result until the fabric had been dressed.

The yarn mixtures I use have a natural fibre content which needs damp pressing. When they are combined with acrylic, which the manufacturers recommend should not be pressed at all, problems can arise. I remember reading in the *To and Fro* magazine what Raymonde Chessum had to say on the subject: 'All yarns can be pressed or damp pressed. They may be ruined in the process but they will press.' Never was there a truer word.

Only experience will tell you which yarns to mix. Yarn purchased from any of the established mail order specialists of machine knitting yarns, local dealers and suppliers is ideal. Mix anything which produces the texture, colour and thickness you require. To test for suitability, each sample should be steam pressed, washed and pressed again to check the result. The only reservation I would have would be mixing yarns such as Shetland wool and lambswool in a garment which would require frequent washing.

121

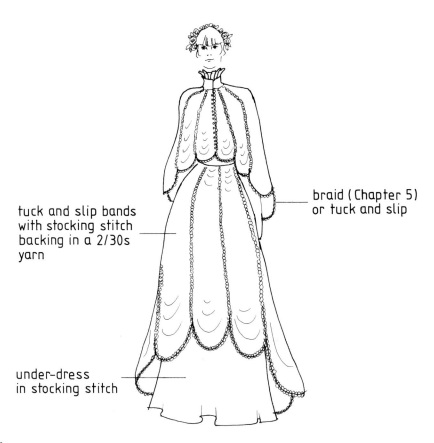

tuck and slip bands
with stocking stitch
backing in a 2/30s
yarn

braid (Chapter 5)
or tuck and slip

under-dress
in stocking stitch

*86 Wedding dress*

# FABRIC DRESSING

1 When the fabric is taken from the machine, pull it lengthwise as usual then gently pull each individual flower lengthwise to set the shape. Do not worry if the flowers are not the same shape. This adds to the interest of the fabric and is one of the features to cultivate. The stripes of flowers are quite formal and cannot be altered. If each individual flower has a slightly different size and shape it helps to make the pattern a little less formal and far more natural (*colour plate 10*).

2 Steam press the lace sections first. The steam will spread and begin to penetrate the slip sections of the fabric. The natural fibre in the yarn should contract slightly with the damp. This sets the stitches of the textured sections which are then steamed on the right side of the fabric. If you have used the 4-ply acrylic crepe it will soften slightly and form its final shape. Should the flowers be too bulky, steam and lightly press from the back of the fabric until the desired effect is achieved.

This treatment should leave you with a surprisingly soft fabric despite the bulk of the flower stripes. There are so many rows knitted in colour using this method that even if you press quite heavily on the slip sections there is still enough bulk to form textured shapes in the fabric.

Figure 86 is a fashion sketch of a wedding dress design which incorporates various tuck and slip features. (*See Chapter 10 for pattern details.*)

122

# 9 Slip shaping on the electronic machine

Because the subject of this book is the use of the slip setting I felt it was important to devote a chapter to automatic shaping using slip. Although automatic shaping is only possible on electronic machines, with the exception of the ruffles in Chapter 5, I do hope that owners of the standard 24-stitch punchcard machines will read on. Guidance is included on knitting these garments on any machine which has a holding position. The only difference is the method of knitting, in that one is manual and the other one is automatic. All the other points apply. Any knitter who has not experimented with this type of sideways knitting would be missing out on an intriguing way of producing garments. I intend to concentrate on skirts as I have knitted so many over the years with varying degrees of success. Maybe the reader can gain from my experience.

Inspiration on this aspect of skirt shaping was first given by Sara Brooks in her book *Garment Shaping Electronically*. I have always wanted to shape garments, particularly skirts, automatically. This book showed the way. The reason only electronic machines are capable of automatic shaping is that the 60-stitch pattern span and the widther button give us the ability to control the whole of the needlebed by mylar sheet.

Understanding the mylar sheet, whatever type of machine you use, is the key to success. The explanation which follows is in diagram form. Written explanations take up too much space. The use of diagrams to explain different methods of producing patterns is long overdue. The British knitter could

gain far more information from foreign magazines if they were prepared to come to terms with diagrams, as 70% of knowledge is gained by vision. Diagrams are international – they require hardly any explanation other than the measurements and the stitch pattern used.

Over the years the import of Japanese magazines has helped to overcome the resistance to diagrams because of the beautiful designs contained in their pages. If we use this momentum, together with the use of international symbols, then there will come a time when knitting patterns, in their present form, will not be needed, leaving room for more designs in the same space.

The mylar sheet markings for electronic machines are quite easy to understand. The skirt used here as an example has only two shaping movements in each half wedge which makes it simpler to explain (*colour plate 12*). Once the mylar sheet markings are understood, anyone with any type of machine should be able to use the patterns without further explanation. See Figs. 87 and 88 for the following explanations.

## RIDGED SKIRT

### All machines

This design is a simple and effective way of knitting a skirt. As only four complete rows are knitted between each shaped section the garment is knitted as a

| MYLAR SHEET | ELECTRONIC MACHINES | PUNCHCARD MACHINES |
|---|---|---|
| 1 square (horizontally) | 2 stitches | 2 stitches |
| 1 square (vertically) | 1 row | 1 row |
| Marked squares | The needles will slip | The needles will be in HP |
| Blank squares | The needles will knit | The needles will knit |

*87 Comparison chart*

pleated skirt. By changing the thickness of the yarn whenever a straight section is reached, a most interesting effect is produced. The fact that there are only two shapings across the width of the needles in work means that lots of panels must be knitted before the hip measurement is reached.

**1 Yarn**

The skirt is knitted using combinations of yarn approximately 2/30s, 2/24s, 2/20s or 2/16s thickness.

> A medium thickness: 2 strands of fine yarn
>
> B thin yarn: 1 strand of fine yarn
>
> C thick yarn: 6 strands of fine yarn
>
> D for waistband: 3 strands of fine yarn

The original 2/24s yarn which was used for the design is no longer available but the principle still applies. The medium yarn should be at least twice the thickness of the fine yarn. The thick yarn should be as thick as the machine will take on the same tension used for the medium yarn. Six strands of 2/24s wool were used for the original garment. This was only possible because of the softness of the yarn. If you are using cotton or any other type of hard yarn, three or four strands may be all that is needed.

The yarn used in the skirt in colour plate 12 is a mixture of natural and man-made fibres. Yarn A is one strand of Hobby with a strand of 2/30s cotton (Silky could be used instead). Yarn B is one strand of 2/30s cotton (Silky would make a good substitute).

Yarn C is a combination of yarns A and B plus one strand of 4-ply acrylic crepe.

At the time of writing my supply of 2/24s and 2/16s wool together with 2/30s cotton is in danger of drying up. Knitters have been lured away from these top-quality fine yarns in the belief that they are too expensive. This is not true. The yardage in a 250-gram cone of 2/30s yarn is four times that of a standard 4-ply and it may cost only twice as much.

If we are not careful, fine yarn will disappear as it has in Japan and all we shall be left with will be standard yarns the thickness of which will be dictated by the spinners. There is a use for each thickness of yarn and it would be a pity to lose any of them. With a standard thickness the yarn content and colour is decided for us. Fine yarn enables us to create our own colour, thickness and texture.

**2 The pleat sequence**

The pleat sequence without shaping consists of eight rows:

> 2 rows yarn A
>
> 2 rows yarn B
>
> 2 rows yarn A
>
> 2 rows yarn C

Use this sequence of yarn changes on a normal-size tension piece to find out the stitch size which is required and to test whether the yarns you have selected will form pleats with a good definition. If not, try adding or subtracting a strand until you are

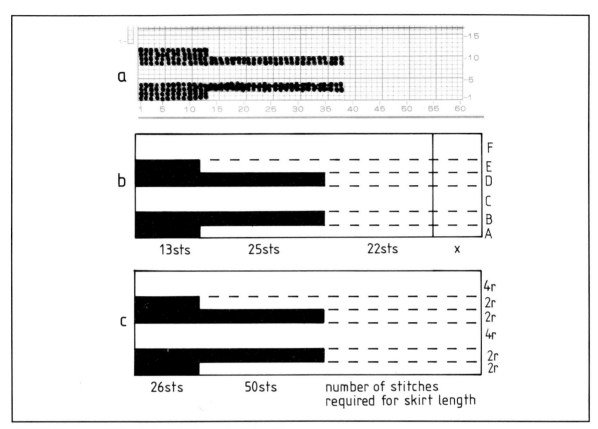

*88 Skirt diagrams: a Mylar sheet    b Mylar sheet with invisible hem (x)    c The skirt as it appears on the needlebed*

satisfied. It will not give you any idea of the finished length of the skirt but does give a trial run to see whether the yarns are running smoothly or not and whether the mix you have chosen is correctly balanced.

The pleat sequence with shaping consists of 16 rows:

5 rows yarn A

2 rows yarn B

6 rows yarn A

2 rows yarn C

1 row yarn A

All the shaping is done with yarn A which is the main yarn. The waist edge of the skirt has the eight-row pleat sequence, the centre section has the 12 rows and the hem edge has the 16-row pleat sequence. There are twice as many rows at the hem edge as there are at the waist.

**3 Tension**

a The tension remains the same throughout the knitting.

b Select a tension which allows the thickest yarn (yarn C) to knit smoothly without snagging or pulling. If the machine is hard to push then your yarn is too thick or the tension is too tight.

125

The above points apply to the principle of knitting the skirt on all types of machine. The following sections illustrate the different methods required by each pattern system to produce identical garments.

| Electronic | Manual |
|---|---|
| 1 Automatic selection by mylar sheet | Manual selection |
| 2 Set to pattern | Leave plain |
| 3 Set to slip | Set to hold |
| 4 Selected needles knit | Non-selected needles knit |

## Electronic machines

When these skirts were first knitted on the 910 it was thought that only 120 needles could be controlled on the Knitmaster 500 and 560 which restricted the length of the skirt. Now, thanks to Doris Coutts who first published the idea in *To and Fro*, a method has been worked out. The technique differs a little from the original idea by Sara Brook but it works well on both patterning systems and is easily adapted to other skirt designs. Each type of electronic machine needs to be set up in a different way.

### Knitmaster 500 and 560

1 Button 1, RH light on, to ensure that the blank sections of the mylar sheet will knit when the machine is set to slip. With this button in use *any needles* outside the point cams will knit when the carriage is set to slip.

2 Button 4 on, pattern width set to 60.

3 NIC 76 at the left of the needlebed, left PC behind NIC and the right PC 120 needles away (between 44 and 45) at the right of the needlebed.

### Brother 910 and 950

1 Buttons 3 and 6 in upper position.

2 Pattern selector button in upper position.

3 Programme: 1–16; 1–60; Fnp Y76–Y76–Y1.

# KNITTING HINTS

## Electronic machines

1 Always knit to the end of the row because the slip cams are in operation and all the needles are in the cam slots under the carriage.

2 Long sections of needles are slipped. When the carriage is returned the needles move slightly forwards to slot into the cams which can cause the yarn to catch. To avoid this lift the yarn above the needles on the Brother 910 and 950. Hold the yarn down with the Knitmaster 500 and 560.

3 Before you begin to knit the skirt make certain that the point cams (Knitmaster) are placed 120 needles apart, and that the programming (Brother) is correct. The first skirt I made using this method had one stitch slipping instead of knitting. The reason? I had 121 needles in the pattern! The numbers of needles to be included in the pattern is inclusive and that is why the mistake was made.

## Manual

### Punchcard machines

1 To ease selection and speed up the work, mark the solid edge of the 1 × 1 pusher with indelible ink on the 25-stitch mark.

2 It is usual on manually selected garments to wrap the yarn to produce a neater fabric. I have not bothered to build this into the electronic design but if you wish to follow tradition then the easiest way is to use automatic wrap.

Follow the instructions for the manually selected skirt but push to holding position one stitch fewer than instructed. Knit one row to the left. At the same side as the carriage push one needle to holding position, knit one row. Repeat throughout the garment. After a while the movement becomes second nature.

. . . . . . . . . . . . . . . . . . . . . . . . . . . . . . . . . . . . . . . . . . . . . . . . . . . . . . . . . .

## Passap machines

1  The number of stitches required for the skirt length means that the lock enters the colour-change area every time it is at the right-hand side of the machine. Make sure that you disconnect the colour changer if it is not to be used. Failure to do so will mean that there will be a couple of rows of waste yarn or the whole lot will fall off because there is no yarn in the feeder.

2  It is not practical on the Passap to disconnect the row counter and reconnect when the straight sections have been reached (as advised for the basic skirt), especially if you use edge springs. The row-count tripper rests against the edge spring and is difficult to disengage. Virtually all the needlebed is being used which means that the row counter is activated whatever its position on the rail.

| PATTERN SECTION | AUTOMATIC SELECTION<br>Electronic | MANUAL SELECTION<br>Punchcard machines |
|---|---|---|
| CAST ON | Cast on in WY over 76/75 sts. Knit a few rows. COL. | Cast on in WY over 76/75 sts. Knit a few rows. COL. |
| SETTING UP THE PANEL | Change to yarn A. Set the carriage to memorize the pattern. Knit 1 row COR. RC 000. Set the carriage to slip. | Change to yarn A. Knit 1 row. COR. RC 000. |
| SECTION A + B<br>First half of wedge | 1  26 needles at the left to slip. Disconnect the row counter. Knit 2 rows<br>2  50 more needles, at the left, to slip. Knit 2 rows. | 1  Set the carriage to hold. Disconnect the row counter. Push to HP 26 needles at the left of the needlebed. Knit 2 rows<br>2  Push to HP 50 needles at the left of needlebed. Knit 2 rows. COR. |
| SECTION C<br>Straight section | 1  All the needles to knit. Reconnect the row counter. Knit 1 row to the left. RC 001.<br>2  Change to yarn B. Knit 2 rows.<br>3  Change to yarn A. Knit 1 row, to the right. RC 004. | 1  Release hold. Reconnect the row counter. Knit 1 row to the left. RC 001.<br>2  Change to yarn B. Knit 2 rows.<br>3  Change to yarn A. Knit 1 row to the right. RC 004. |
| SECTIONS D and E<br>Second half of wedge | 1  76 needles at the left to slip. Disconnect the row counter. Knit 2 rows.<br>2  26 needles to slip at the left of needlebed. Knit 2 rows. | 1  Disconnect the row counter. Set machine to hold. Push to HP 76 needles at the left. Knit 2 rows.<br>2  Push 50 needles, nearest those in WP, from HP to UWP. Knit 2 rows. COR. |
| SECTION F<br>Second straight section | 1  All needles to knit. COR. Reconnect the row counter, knit 1 row to the left. RC 005.<br>2  Change to yarn C. Knit 2 rows.<br>3  Change to yarn A. Knit 1 row to the right. RC 008. | 1  Release hold. Reconnect the row counter. Knit 1 row to the left. RC 005.<br>2  Change to yarn C. Knit 2 rows.<br>3  Change to yarn A. Knit 1 row to the right. RC 008. |
| END OF FIRST PLEAT | Repeat, from section A + B to section F, 4 times more. RC 40. Strip off with WY. | Repeat, from section A + B to section F, 4 times more. RC 40. Strip off with WY. |

*89 Knitting instructions for sample panel of ridged skirt*

127

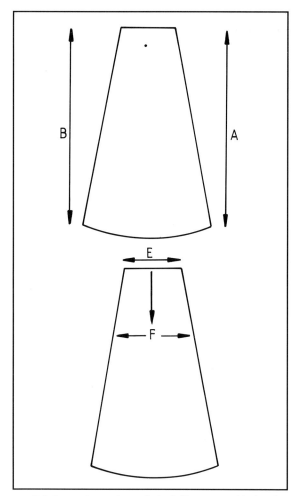

*90 Calculations for a sideways-knitted skirt pattern: skirt length (top) and skirt width (bottom)*

# Calculations for a sideways-knitted skirt pattern

When designing a pattern for a skirt a decision has to be made as to how wide the skirt is to be at the hip. This has to be predetermined. No matter how carefully the panels are measured, until the skirt has been pressed and washed there is always the chance that your calculations will not produce quite the fit you wanted. The fabric which tumbles off the knitting machine in no way represents the finished

article. The only way to understand exactly what happens to the fabric is to knit a sample panel using the knitting instructions given in Fig. 89. Follow the instructions in Chapter 1 (*Tension guide*) for washing and pressing.

## To work out the skirt length

Measure the length of the sample panel (A). Divide the number of stitches by the length of the sample (B) to find out how many stitches to each centimetre (C) and multiply C by the length of skirt you require (D).

Formula for skirt length (*refer to Fig. 90, top*):

$$A \div B = C$$
$$C \times D = \text{number of stitches to be cast on for the skirt length}$$

I feel it is important to knit a skirt a little longer than you require. This will give you a seam allowance to join the waistband and also allow for any variations of length which occur when the actual skirt is knitted. There is no need for a hem allowance. Sometimes the weight of the fabric and the water temperature when you wash the complete garment can alter the length of the skirt. If it turns out too long it can be shortened with cut-and-sew or the surplus can be enclosed in the waistband. If it is too short the only thing to do is to re-knit the whole thing.

## To work out the width

To work out the number of rows needed for the hip measurement, measure across the panel about 10–15 cms (4–6 in.) from the top (F). Divide this measurement into the number of rows knitted (E) to obtain the number of rows to each centimetre (inch) (G). Multiply G by the number of centimetres (inches) required for the hip measurement + 5 cms (2 in.) (H). Round it up or down to the nearest eight rows so that you are knitting complete panels.

Formula for calculating the width of the skirt (*refer to Fig. 90, bottom*):

$$E \div F = G$$
$$G \times H = \text{number of rows to be knitted for the hips}$$

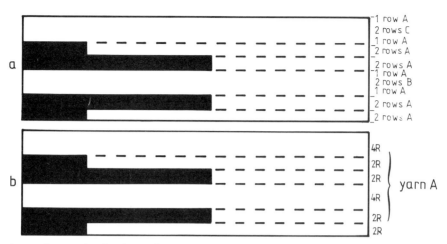

*91 a Ridge pleat with yarn changes   b ridge pleat without yarn changes*

# Box pleats

Using exactly the same mylar sheet it is possible to create box pleats. All that is required is to change the yarn in a different sequence. The thickness of the yarn is crucial. A thick yarn always moves towards the purl side of the fabric. A thin yarn always moves to the knit side. Learning where to place these yarns is most important. Work the following:

1 One ridge pleat (*Fig. 91a*).

2 One full pleat with no yarn change (*Fig. 91b*).

3 One ridge pleat in reverse, i.e. exchange yarns B and C.

4 One full pleat with no yarn change.

Repeat for the required length (hip size).

The fabric produced by using the above sequence is reversible. There are lots of ways of adapting these pleats without alteration to the mylar sheet or, in the case of manual patterning, to the needle selection.

### Box pleat variations

1 Colour can be introduced when the yarn thickness is changed.

2 Box pleats with patterning on the knit side.

Patterning can be introduced in section 4 of the box pleat. The pattern must be one which uses the knit side as the right side. Lace, punch lace, Fair Isle or petal slip stitch are all suitable settings. There is no need to shape this section. As long as the pattern is wide enough to cover the fold in the box pleat at each side and adds approximately 2 cm ($\frac{3}{4}$ in.) to the length of the knitting, the pleats will fall correctly. Figure 92 illustrates the use of lace as a surface pattern.

3 Box pleats with patterning on the purl side.

*92 Lace pleats*

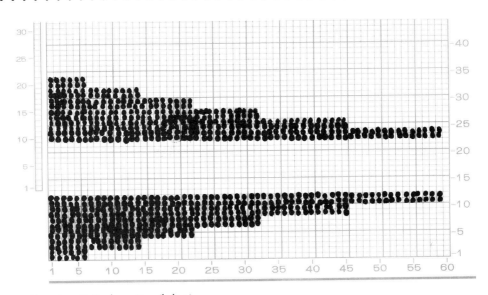

93 *Skirt pattern* (above)    94 *Raglan pattern* (below)

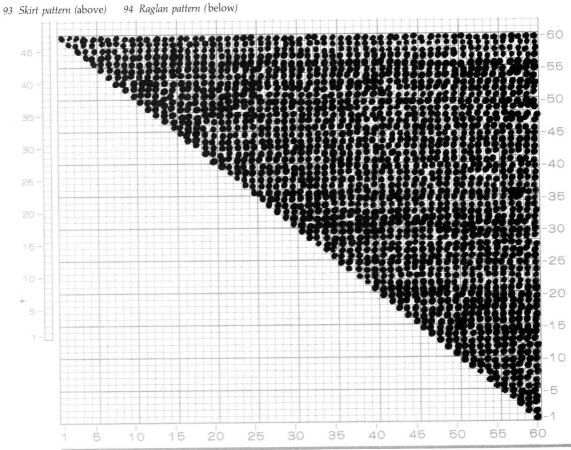

Work as above but knit the pattern in section 2. Suitable pattern settings are weave, tuck and slip.

Changing the yarn in a different sequence alters the type of pleat which is produced. See whether you can work a knife pleat.

## MYLAR SHEET VARIATIONS

1 Figure 93 is a mylar sheet design for a skirt based on the same principle as the ridged design. There are 12 rows of shaping and 10 rows straight between each half wedge. Use the information given at the beginning of the chapter to translate the mylar sheet markings into a garment.

2 Once you have done this, using only one yarn, try changing the yarn thickness in the ten straight rows to produce yet another type of pleated skirt (*colour plates 3 and 9*). Remember, the greater the contrast between the yarn thicknesses the more definite the pleats.

Use the same principle for knitting skirts on chunky machines. With half the number of stitches and rows they do not take long to knit. Mock pleats can be knitted by threading two yarns into the yarn feeder, a thin one into the plating feeder and a thicker one into feeder 1. When a straight section is reached, remove the thick yarn from the feeder for two rows. Replace, knit two rows with both yarns and repeat. Continue with the next shaping, and so on, for the required length.

# RAGLAN SHAPING ELECTRONICALLY

The mylar sheet in Fig. 94 is designed for that purpose. The garment is knitted sideways, all in one piece, in a similar way to the skirts. Side seams and underarm allowances need to be built in (*Fig. 95*). Using a mylar sheet enables us to work the shapings automatically.

Each square on the mylar sheet represents two stitches and two rows. The sheet is not the only way

of knitting these garments but as it can be used by both electronic patterning systems it seems best to stick to this method.

The one design gives enough rows and stitches for most garments which are knitted in a fine yarn. Work a normal tension piece and calculate the number of stitches needed for the armhole.

The armhole depth is the critical part of the design. Do make sure that it is at least one-quarter of the chest measurement plus ease. This ensures that the garment is a comfortable fit.

If 90 stitches are needed for the armhole then the mylar sheet, on the Knitmaster machines, is marked with the designer pencil, in column 2, for a slow return on row 45.

Brother machines are programmed to include 45 rows with the number 5 (reflection) button up. This is because the machine is set to knit every row twice; e.g. $2 \times 45 = 90$. Each yarn type and tension will require a different number of rows and therefore a fresh mark on the sheet, or re-programming. Remember, the number of rows you knit will be the same as the number of stitches required for the shaping.

To simplify the knitting of the garment, set up all the shaped sections on either the right or the left side of the needlebed. Figure 95 illustrates, in diagram form, the order in which the garment is knitted. All the shaping takes place on the right-hand side of the needlebed and the needles at the left are always in use.

## KNITTING DETAILS

### Electronic raglan shaping

1 When sections A and B have been knitted the pattern sheet is disconnected and the machine is set to hold. Push all the needles which were slipping to HP.

2 Knit sections C, D and E on the remaining needles.

3 Release hold, reconnect the pattern sheet and knit one row to the right to return all needles to their correct working position, i.e. most of the needles at the right of the centre are slipping.

131

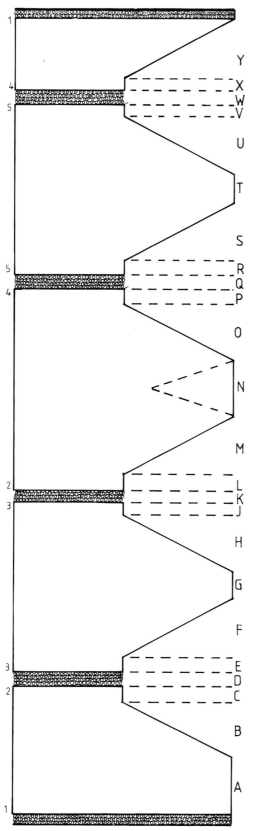

Continue to knit and you will see that as the sheet knits in reverse, two more needles will be automatically returned to normal working position. Follow the above instructions using the notes and the diagram to complete the garment.

When the garment is released from the machine and has been pressed, cut the waste yarn sections D, K, Q and W, in half. Take care that you do not cut the main yarn – otherwise the garment will be ruined.

Add the cuffs and welts (*see Chapter 10 for details*). Graft the seams matching points 1 to 1, 2 to 2, 3 to 3, etc.

## Pattern notes

1 To avoid having to calculate the front neck shaping (section N) use a standard neck shaping on your charting device and follow this.

2 If the yarn is knitting in where it should be slipping, see note 2 under Knitting hints on page 126 in the skirt section.

95  *One-piece raglan top*
    Cast on in WY

| | | |
|---|---|---|
| ⅔ of back | ⎧ Y | Back neck |
| | ⎨ X | 1st raglan shaping for back |
| | ⎩ W | Underarm seam |
| | V | 20 rows WY |
| Sleeve | ⎧ U | Underarm seam |
| | ⎪ T | 1st raglan shaping for sleeve |
| | ⎨ S | Top of sleeve |
| | ⎪ R | 2nd raglan shaping for sleeve |
| | ⎩ Q | Underarm seam |
| | P | 20 rows WY |
| Front | ⎧ O | Underarm seam |
| | ⎪ N | 1st raglan shaping for front |
| | ⎨ M | Front neck |
| | ⎪ L | 2nd raglan shaping for front |
| | ⎩ K | Underarm seam |
| | J | 20 rows WY |
| Sleeve | ⎧ H | Underarm seam |
| | ⎪ G | 1st raglan shaping for sleeve |
| | ⎨ F | Top of second sleeve |
| | ⎪ E | 2nd raglan shaping for sleeve |
| | ⎩ D | Underarm seam |
| | C | 20 rows WY |
| ⅓ of back | ⎧ B | Underarm seam |
| | ⎨ A | 2nd raglan shaping for back |
| | Strip off in WY | |

direction
of knitting

stocking stitch

mock pleats

thick yarn

fine yarn

mosaic design

box pleats

*96 Mock-pleated dress and box pleats with mosaic*

3 Use textured, random or space-dyed yarns to add interest to the garment. Patterning is possible used in conjunction with this method of shaping but unless it is organized carefully confusion can occur on the raglan shapings.

4 The pattern is drawn with the sleeves the same length as the bodice. Sleeves of a different length can be knitted by adding or subtracting stitches after section C and section Q have been worked. Remember to return the needles to the correct number after the sleeves have been knitted.

The explanation for knitting this type of garment is much harder to write about than to do. Select some fine cheap yarn and test the method before you knit a sweater with expensive yarn.

If you have a punchcard machine you can follow the outline of the method, putting into use the knowledge gained at the beginning of the chapter. There is no restriction on the number of stitches which are used for shaping as you are doing it manually. The method is an easy way of knitting a raglan shaping without having to join all the seams.

Figure 96 shows two examples of garments which can be made using automatic shaping. (*See Chapter 10 for pattern details.*)

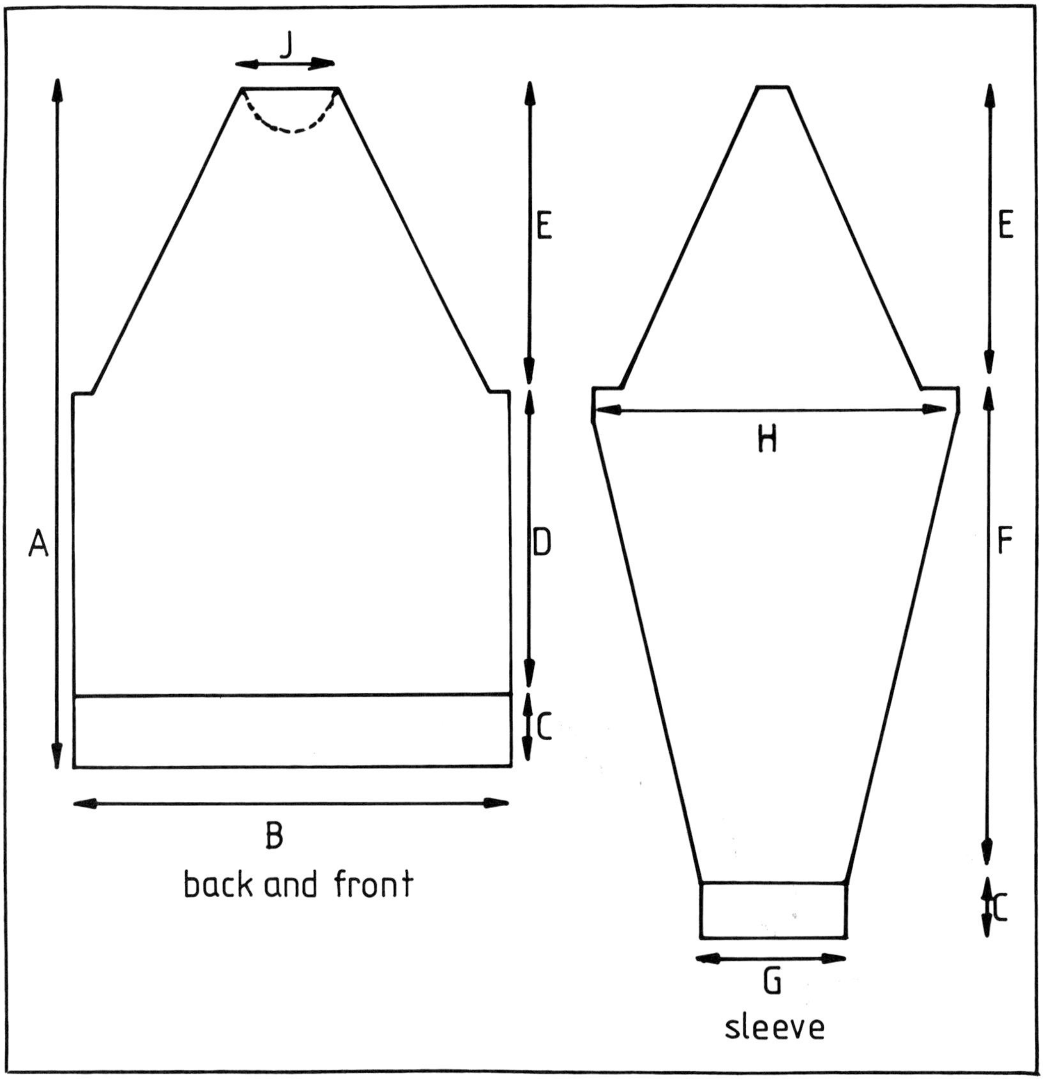

J

E

A

D

C

B

back and front

E

H

F

C

G

sleeve

# 10 Basic patterns

This chapter contains a set of basic garment shapes. They have been simplified so that they can be adjusted to suit your own particular requirements. Details of the fashion ideas which are featured throughout the book are also included. I have avoided giving specific instructions for each garment as the stitch patterns and yarns are interchangeable. Where unusual techniques have been used, full details are given. The diagrams should be used as basic shapes which can be altered to suit any figure type. The measurements included are for loose fitting, medium-sized garments to give you a basis from which to work. Clothes these days are not as fitted as they used to be and as a general rule I find that, for garments without shaping, one size is sufficient for most people. Alterations to the basic measurements will only be required by someone who is at either end of the sizing charts or who needs a more fitted or indeed a looser garment.

97 *Raglan sweater*
A  63.5 cm (25 in.)
B  53.5 cm (21 in.)
C  7.5 cm (3 in.)
D  30.5 cm (12 in.)
E  25.5 cm (10 in.)
F  46 cm (18 in.)
G  23 cm (9 in.)
H  41 cm (16 in.)
J  15.5 cm (6 in.)

## CLASSIC RAGLAN SWEATER (*Chapter 2, Fig. 9*)

This design is knitted in a simple stitch pattern (*Fig. 97*).

## TAM-O'-SHANTER, SCARF AND GLOVES (*Chapter 3, Fig. 30*)

This cannot be called a basic pattern. It took a good three months to perfect and I have included more pattern details than in the other designs (*Fig. 98*). The yarn used was Forsell's 2-ply used double.

### Tam-o'-shanter

The number of rows to knit is determined by the diameter of the 'tam', usually 24–27 cm ($9\frac{1}{2}$–$10\frac{1}{2}$ in.). The radius of the circle (half the diameter) is multiplied by the number of rows to each centimetre. Therefore, using a tension sample with a scale of 33 rows to 10 cm (4 in.), a 'tam' of 27 cm ($10\frac{1}{2}$ in.) diameter would need 3.3 × 13.5 = 44.55 or 45 rows.

The number of stitches required for each piece is half the circumference of the circle, i.e. 3.142 × the radius, multiplied by the number of stitches to each centimetre. Therefore, using a tension sample with a

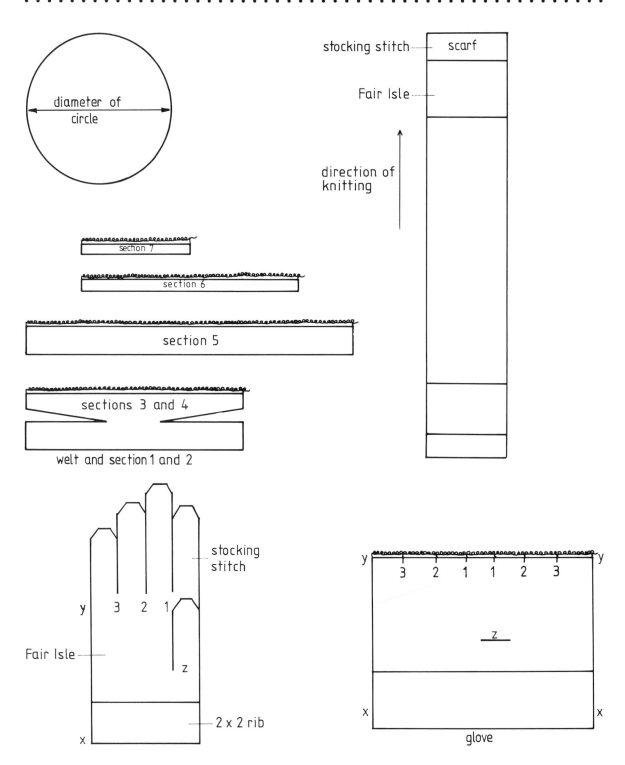

diameter of
circle

stocking stitch—— scarf

Fair Isle——

direction of
knitting

section 7

section 6

section 5

sections 3 and 4

welt and section 1 and 2

stocking
stitch

y    3  2  1

z

Fair Isle——

2 x 2 rib

x

y            y
   3  2  1  1  2  3

z

x                x

glove

*98  Tam-o'-shanter, scarf and gloves (not to scale)*
    *Tam-o'-shanter: diameter of circle 27 cm (10½ in.)*
    *Scarf: length 140 cm (55 in.)  width 32 cm (12½ in.)*
    *Gloves (measurements for guidance only):*
        *Index finger  7 cm (2¾ in.)*
        *2nd finger  8.25 cm (3¼ in.)*
        *3rd finger  7.5 cm (3 in.)*
        *Little finger  5.75 cm (2¼ in.)*
        *Palm (width)  19 cm (7½ in.)*
        *Base of fingers to wrist  16.5 cm (6½ in.)*

scale of 31 stitches to 10 cm (4 in.) a 'tam' of 27 cm (10½ in.) diameter would need $3.142 \times 13.5 \times 3.1 = 131.49 = 132$ stitches (actual stitches used = 134). The number of stitches has to be adjusted to make sure that the pattern will match. The rows can be adjusted so that the centre of the circle is neat and tight.

## SECTIONS 1 AND 2

### Two pieces in double rib

Each piece measures half the circumference of the circle.

Cast on in WY 67/67 stitches. Knit a few rows.

Change to MY and TD6. Knit 4 rows.

Transfer for 2 × 2 rib, TD 3/3. Knit 61 rows.

Transfer to back bed, TD6. Knit 4 rows stocking stitch.

Pick up first row knitted. Knit 3 rows.

Strip off with WY.

## SECTIONS 3 AND 4

### Two pieces in Fair Isle

Replace the ribbing onto the needles with the purl side facing the machine. TD8. Shape a curve at the centre of each piece by pushing 21 stitches to HP, at the opposite side to the carriage, 4 times in all. Work the Fair Isle using PP44. Transfer EAN along the row (*see pattern details*).

## SECTION 5

Replace both pieces of fabric onto the needlebed with the right side facing the machine (68/67 stitches with 2 on the centre needle). TD6, knit PP45. Transfer EAN along the row as before.

## SECTION 6

Replace the remaining stitches onto the needlebed. Increase 1st at left (35/34 sts). Knit either PP44 or PP46 with the card locked. Transfer EAN along the row as before.

## SECTION 7

Replace the remaining stitches onto the needlebed. TD2. Knit 5 rows stocking stitch.

Break off the yarn leaving a long end, thread a tapestry needle and, with the yarn double, take from the machine onto the needle and thread. Pull up tightly and secure. Join seams.

*Note*  Each time the stitches are reduced and the waste yarn is inserted, disconnect the row counter. Reconnect when the next section is knitted so that you have a record of the number of rows knitted.

Fit the 'tam' over a plate of a similar size and steam well. Leave to dry. Thread a piece of elastic through the double rib and adjust to fit the head.

## Scarf (approximately 140 cm long and 16 cm wide when stitched – 55 in. × 6 in.)

The Fair Isle band is placed 25 rows from the cast-on edge so that the full design can be seen. Remember to turn the punchcard upside down when you reach the end – otherwise the pattern will be upside down.

Use Forsell's 2-ply yarn, TD7 on the Brother and $7\frac{2}{3}$ on the Knitmaster. Mark every 50th row with contrast yarn to speed up the finishing. After releasing from the machine give the scarf a steam press. Fold the fabric in half. With the right sides together match the contrast yarn and join on the sewing machine using a stretch stitch. Attach a fringe through the double thickness of fabric to finish.

Use the card in Fig. 15 to knit the scarf shown in colour plate 2.

## Gloves

Gloves on the knitting machine are very easy. In this pattern the fingers are knitted circular using the ribber. If you have no ribber then knit the fingers on the single bed, halving the number of rows. A glove pattern can be made to measure in the same way as a garment.

Measure round the palm of the hand (y–y). Add one stitch each side for the seam. Measure the length of the palm, from the base of the finger (y) to the wrist (x), to determine how many rows need to be knitted. (A deep rib of 40 rows gives a cosy fit around the wrist.)

### KNITTING INSTRUCTIONS FOR GLOVES

#### Palm

Knit the rib and half the number of Fair Isle rows. Knit by hand, onto a nylon cord, 8 stitches at either the left or right of the centre, depending on which glove is being knitted. Knit the other half of the Fair Isle rows then one row in stocking stitch. Strip off with WY.

#### Fingers

Push up the ribber bed. Set on H for tubular knitting.

*Index finger*  Fold the fabric in half and pick up 7 stitches each side of the fold, 7 onto the main bed and 7 onto the ribber (*section 1–1 in Fig. 98*). Push one needle on each bed to WP at the left of these needles. Knit 50 rows circular.

On both beds dec 1 st at each side. Knit 2 rows. Repeat once more.

Transfer stitches to the main bed. Knit 1 row. Cast off.

Repeat for all the fingers, picking up the stitches from the relevant sections and knitting the required number of rows before shaping the top.

*2nd finger*   7 sts each bed + 1 st from the base of the previous finger. Knit 56 rows.

*3rd finger*   7 sts + 1: Knit 50 rows.

*Little finger*   6 sts + 1: Knit 44 rows.

The *thumb* is picked up from the 8 stitches knitted in nylon cord. 8 sts on one bed, 8 sts on the other bed plus 1 extra stitch on each bed: Knit 50 rows.

## SLIPOVER

### (*Chapter 3, Fig. 30*)

This slipover is easy to knit. Use it as a stitch sampler. It is an ideal way of testing a new stitch idea. No shaping is involved (*Fig. 99*).

There are various ways of knitting these garments.

1  Knit two pieces alike from hip to shoulder. Join the shoulder seams. Work the armholes before joining the side seams.

2  Knit from the hip, over the shoulder then back to the hip.

3  Knit the top sideways. Verticals stripes look effective.

Work the armbands before joining the side seams. Crochet or knit the neck edge to neaten.

The patterns on the back and front are slightly different but as no one can possibly see both sides at the same time it is not likely that it will be noticed.

Try using the poppy punchcard (*Fig. 100*) which has been adapted to 24 stitches. PP43E on pattern sheet 8 has the alternating poppy which adds to the interest of the fabric. The slip rows have been increased to 20. The poppy top in colour plate 5 was made extra wide to show off the stitch to best advantage. Care should be taken when knitting a

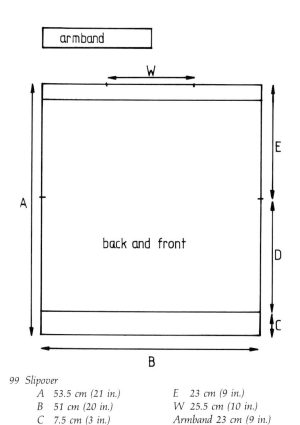

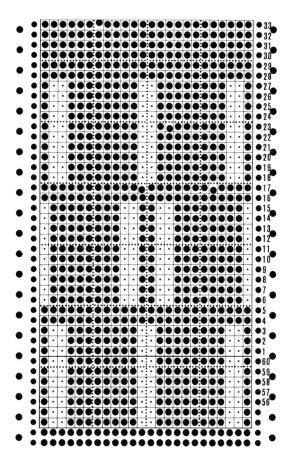

**99 Slipover**

| | |
|---|---|
| A  53.5 cm (21 in.) | E   23 cm (9 in.) |
| B  51 cm (20 in.) | W  25.5 cm (10 in.) |
| C  7.5 cm (3 in.) | Armband 23 cm (9 in.) |
| D  23 cm (9 in.) | |

**100 Poppy punchcard**

garment in this type of slip stitch that the ribbing does indeed pull in the welt. The garment in Fig. 32 was knitted in the conventional way and it is obvious from the photograph that the rib is too wide. To overcome this difficulty, cast on above the welt and knit the front and back before adding the welt (see the pattern details).

## PETAL SLIP STITCH JACKET

### (*Chapter 4, Fig. 38*)

The jacket is based on rectangles (*Fig. 101*). Petal slip stitch has motifs which lend themselves very well to this type of design. Instead of working a standard tension piece it is easier to work in motifs.

Work a sample of petal slip stitch using the punchcard in Fig. 35 following experiment 5 on page 56 (with the stripes), in the yarn of your choice. Measure the height and width of a single motif and calculate how many are needed for the width and length of the garment.

Always work in complete or half motifs. Any shaping is worked between them. It may be necessary to add some stitches in order to have complete flowers but it is more important to keep the design correct than to worry about a few extra stitches.

The pattern for a garment with a motif measuring 6.7 cm across and 10.5 cm deep ($2\frac{1}{2}$ in. × 4 in.) would read as follows.

139

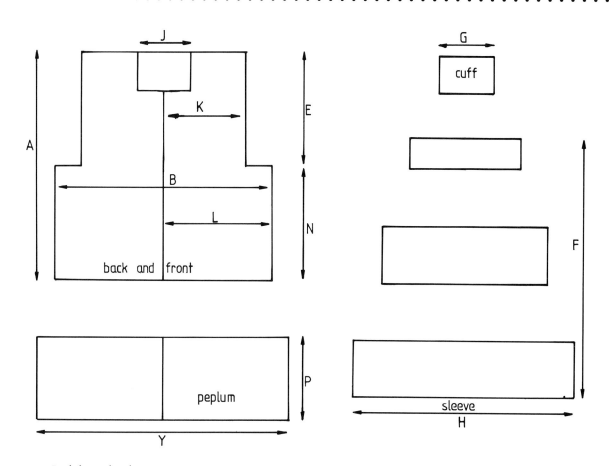

*101 Petal slip stitch jacket*

| | | | |
|---|---|---|---|
| A | 53.5 cm (21 in.) | J | 14 cm (5½ in.) |
| B | 63.5 cm (25 in.) | K | 17.5 cm (7 in.) |
| E | 26.25 cm (10½ in.) | L | 32 cm (12½ in.) |
| F | 52.5 cm (20 in.) | N | 26.25 cm (10½ in.) |
| G | 19 cm (7½ in.) | P | 11 cm (4½ in.) |
| H | 56 cm (22 in.) | Y | 56 cm (22 in.) |

## BACK PEPLUM

Cast on in WY. Knit a few rows.

Change to PY. Work a 5-row hem, i.e. 5 rows, foldline, second 5 rows. Pick up first row knitted in PY.

Work 1 row of 8 motifs, ½ + 7 + ½ motifs + 2 sts. Reduce sts by 24 along the row (see pattern details) to 7 motifs + 2 sts.

## BACK

Replace reduced fabric onto machine.

Work 2 rows of 7 motifs + 2 sts to the armholes.

Cast off over one full motif at the beginning of the next 2 rows. (Armhole shaping complete.)

Work 2 rows of motifs over the remaining 5 motifs × 2 sts.

Mark the back neck, ½ + 1 + ½ motifs. Strip off with WY.

## RIGHT FRONT PEPLUM

Work as for back with 1 row of 4 motifs + 2 sts. Reduce the number of sts by 12 in the same way as before.

## RIGHT FRONT

Replace reduced fabric onto machine.

Work 2 rows over $3\frac{1}{2}$ motifs + 2 sts. (The half motif will be at the centre front.)

Cast off across 1 complete motif at the right of the needlebed. (Armhole shaping complete.)

Work 1 row of motifs over remaining $2\frac{1}{2}$ motifs + 2 sts.

Cast off over 1 full motif (24 sts) at the left. (Front neck shaping worked.)

Work 1 row of motifs over the remaining $1\frac{1}{2}$ motifs. Strip off with WY.

## LEFT FRONT

Repeat as for the right front, reversing the shapings.

## SLEEVE

The sleeve is knitted in three pieces as indicated in Fig. 101, working from the shoulder to the cuff.

Work as for the peplum omitting the 5-row hem.

Cast on in WY. Knit a few rows.

Change to BY, mark the 2 centre motifs $\frac{1}{2} + 1 + \frac{1}{2}$. These stitches are gathered onto the centre 6 needles of the shoulder seam when the garment is finished. Knit 2 rows of motifs. Reduce the stitches to 6 motifs + 2 sts following the instructions.

Replace onto machine. Knit 2 rows of motifs. Reduce to 4 motifs + 2 sts and proceed as before.

Work 1 row of motifs. Over the centre 48 sts transfer the stitch on EAN to its adjacent stitch. Knit 1 row MY.

Strip off with WY. The centre 24 sts are gathered onto the centre 6 needles of the cuff.

This is a simplified pattern. The instructions should

be sufficient to enable you to create your own version. Work all the reducing rows on the centre two rows of the coloured stripes. The result is a garment with virtually invisible shapings and seams which, apart from the peplum seams, match perfectly.

The cherries in Chapter 8 can also be used in the same way using the same measurements. When knitting the sleeves for the cherry jacket, work the sleeves in the conventional way, from cuff to shoulder, as the motif may prove difficult to knit upside-down. The increases are worked in complete motifs to disguise them.

The cherry design is a 12-stitch repeat. Two bunches of cherries are required for each increase. To keep the pattern correct leave all the work in place except the 18 stitches at the extreme edges of the knitting. Push an extra 12 stitches to working position at each side of the needlebed. Spread out the 18 stitches at each side evenly over the extra 12 needles at each side of the work using either a garter bar or a transfer tool. The empty in-between needles can be left empty as they are on the underarm seam at the end of the lace section of the pattern.

Once this type of shaping has been mastered it makes any other way seem rather tedious. The mind is left free to knit complete rows of motifs without having one eye on the row counter. The number of increases or decreases is reduced to a mere handful which in itself is an advantage. Try it and see! The explanation is far more complex than the practice.

# SIDEWAYS-KNITTED TOP WITH YOKE

## (Chapter 4, Fig. 38)

A standard sideways-knitted garment (Fig. 48) can be adapted easily to take a yoke. The simplest way to do this is to mark off, with a compass, a semicircle 18 cm (7 in.) radius to give a yoke 10 cm (4 in.) deep (Fig. 102). The back and front will be the same shape but when the yoke is knitted each piece can be shaped differently to correct the discrepancy.

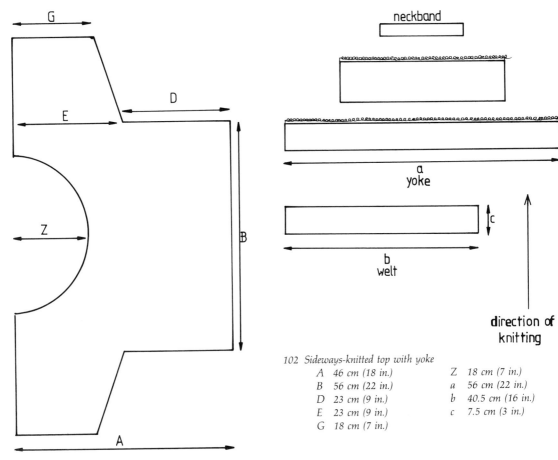

102 *Sideways-knitted top with yoke*

| | | | | |
|---|---|---|---|---|
| A | 46 cm (18 in.) | | Z | 18 cm (7 in.) |
| B | 56 cm (22 in.) | | a | 56 cm (22 in.) |
| D | 23 cm (9 in.) | | b | 40.5 cm (16 in.) |
| E | 23 cm (9 in.) | | c | 7.5 cm (3 in.) |
| G | 18 cm (7 in.) | | | |

## Yoke

The yoke section is composed of straight pieces which are gradually reduced in the same way as the tam-o'-shanter. To calculate the number of stitches and rows needed for the yoke, knit a tension sample and use the formula for the tam'.

### SECTION 1A

The pintucks are worked immediately after the garment is replaced onto the machine. If you have no ribber then make hems instead. Change colour after each pintuck is finished to simplify the picking up. Decrease the stitches by a third if lace or tuck is to be used or by a quarter if Fair Isle or slip has been selected.

### SECTION 2A

The pattern section is worked over the remaining stitches which are reduced again by a half when the section is complete. Replace the remaining stitches onto the needlebed and work the last pintuck section. Reduce the stitches once more for the neck. Aim to reduce the stitches to a figure near to the number required for a standard round neck.

The back yoke is shaped for approximately eight rows, over the whole needlebed after the pintucks have been worked. Repeat after the pattern section but before the stitches are reduced. When the back is picked up for the neckband the stitches are spread evenly over all the needles in work. The front neck stitches are placed on the needles with half the number of stitches placed onto the centre third of the needles in working position. The remaining stitches are placed singly on the needles at each side of the centre to reproduce the normal front neck shaping.

# LONGLINE SWEATER

### (*Chapter 5, Fig. 44*)

A longline sweater with no shaping is best knitted in a fine soft yarn to enable the fabric to drape over the hips (*Fig. 103*). The neck can be shaped whilst the garment is being knitted or shaped by cut-and-sew.

The ruffle is knitted using PP26 or PP27. It looks better on a round neck rather than a V-neck as it tends to be rather rigid.

The flounce, PP47 or PP48, will give a much better drape on a V-neck. Turn the punchcard over for the second side of the neck to ensure that the drape is the same on each side.

A flounce is based on a circle. Instead of the straight edging of the ruffle, with the fullness knitted separately, a flounce is knitted using the same principle as is used to make a circular skirt. The punchcard is designed to introduce a few more stitches every two rows to form the fullness of the hem edge. When a flounce is released from the machine the narrow edge of the fabric forms a curve.

*103  Longline sweater*

| | | | |
|---|---|---|---|
| A | 63.5 cm (25 in.) | F | 43 cm (17 in.) |
| B | 53.5 cm (21 in.) | G | 21.5 cm (8½ in.) |
| D | 38 cm (15 in.) | H | 51 cm (20 in.) |
| E | 25.5 cm (10 in.) | J | 15 cm (6 in.) |

back and front

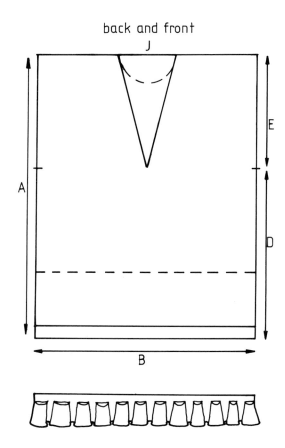

sleeve

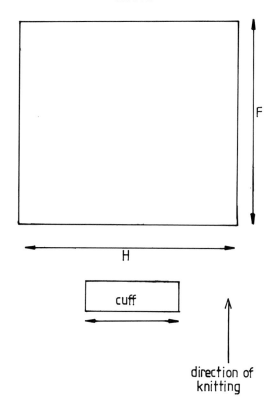

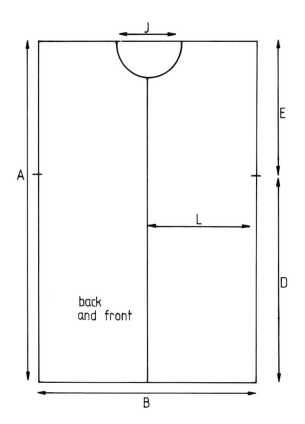

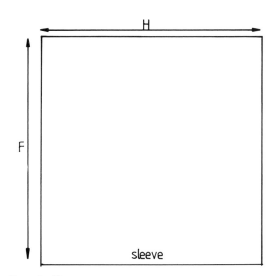

104 Drop-shoulder sweater

| | | | |
|---|---|---|---|
| A | 56 cm (22 in.) | F | 46 cm (18 in.) |
| B | 51 cm (20 in.) | H | 46 cm (18 in.) |
| D | 33 cm (13 in.) | J | 15.5 cm (6 in.) |
| E | 23 cm (9 in.) | L | 25.5 cm (10 in.) |

105 Three-colour design

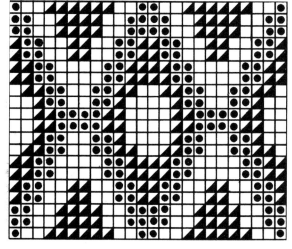

□ colour 1
⊡ colour 2
◤ colour 3

# DROP-SHOULDER JACKET IN DOUBLE-BED FABRIC

### (*Chapter 6, Fig. 58*)

A drop-shoulder shape provides a simple canvas for many of the complicated double-bed slip fabrics described in Chapter 6 (*Fig. 104*).

Ripple stitch or three-colours-in-a-row with a pintucked backing are ideal for these simple, shaped jackets.

The three-colour design in Fig. 105 is a pattern with only 20 rows which would be ideal for an evening jacket. If a lurex thread is added to colour 2, a rich brocade effect is produced with the lurex showing on the top of the pintuck.

144

# DOUBLE JACQUARD COAT

The coat in colour plate 7 is a similar shape to the jacket outlined in Chapter 6. Elongate the side seams to the length required. The hem edge should be approximately 5–10 cm (2–4 in.) wider than the bust measurement. Curve the hem to allow the coat to hang properly.

The coat was knitted in two ends of Forsell's 2/16s yarn using TD5/4 approximately. No problems were encountered with the knitting and the fabric was reasonably soft.

The design in Fig. 76 would make an interesting border. (Use the sky from Fig. 15 to complete the picture.) Knit it in blister stitch for a three-dimensional effect.

# DRESS WITH MULTICOLOURED CENTRE PANEL

(*Chapter 8, Fig. 86*)

This is a simple garment in stocking stitch with a patterned centre panel on the bodice. A similar pattern, in braid, is inserted into the skirt (*colour plate 10 and Fig. 106*).

## BODICE

Knit the two centre panels, in whichever colour sequence you choose, for the required number of rows. PP39 and PP49 are used to alternate the pattern and allow the flowers to slot into each lace zigzag.

The side panels are knitted from the waist, gradually increasing on one side to the shoulder and down the other side, decreasing to the waist. Knit a few rows in waste yarn and repeat for the second side.

## SKIRT

Knit a sample of braid using PP21. Use this to calculate how many flowers are needed for the length of the skirt required. Knit four alike.

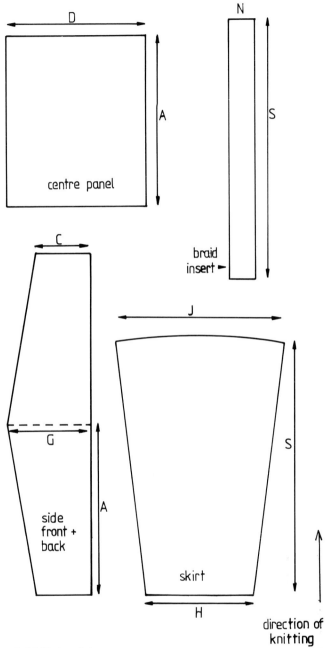

106 *Multicoloured dress*

| | | | |
|---|---|---|---|
| A | 46 cm (18 in.) | H | 19 cm (7½ in.) |
| D | 28 cm (11 in.) | J | 39.5 cm (15½ in.) |
| C | 13 cm (5 in.) | S | 73.5 cm (29 in.) |
| G | 20.5 cm (8 in.) | N | 4 cm (1½ in.) |

145

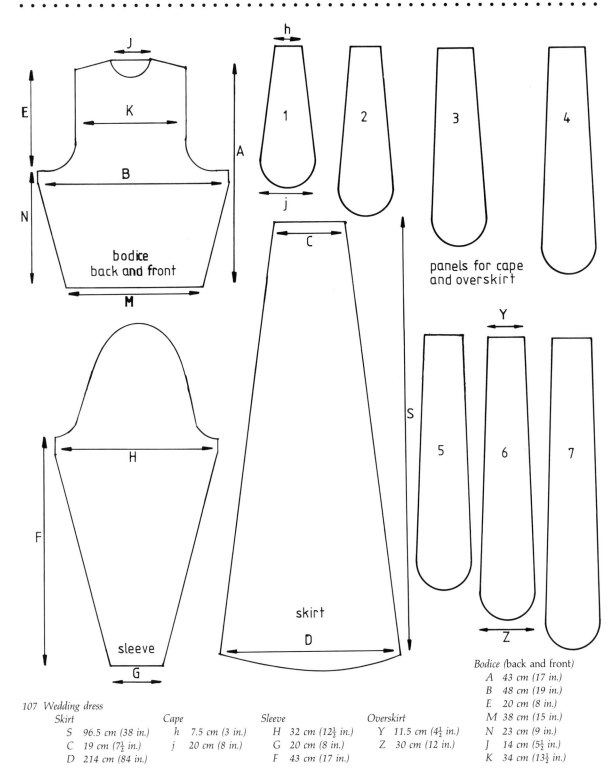

107 Wedding dress

| | | | | | | | | |
|---|---|---|---|---|---|---|---|---|
| **Skirt** | | **Cape** | | **Sleeve** | | **Overskirt** | | **Bodice** (back and front) |
| S | 96.5 cm (38 in.) | h | 7.5 cm (3 in.) | H | 32 cm (12½ in.) | Y | 11.5 cm (4½ in.) | A | 43 cm (17 in.) |
| C | 19 cm (7½ in.) | j | 20 cm (8 in.) | G | 20 cm (8 in.) | Z | 30 cm (12 in.) | B | 48 cm (19 in.) |
| D | 214 cm (84 in.) | | | F | 43 cm (17 in.) | | | E | 20 cm (8 in.) |

Bodice (back and front)
A  43 cm (17 in.)
B  48 cm (19 in.)
E  20 cm (8 in.)
M  38 cm (15 in.)
N  23 cm (9 in.)
J  14 cm (5½ in.)
K  34 cm (13½ in.)

146

The skirt is knitted from top to bottom with a braid insert between each of the four panels. A panelled skirt is based on the waist measurement, unlike the sideways-knitted skirts which are based on a hip measurement.

108 *Box pleats with mosaic pattern*
R    86.5 cm (34 in.)
V    R + pleat shaping
S    73.5 cm (29 in.)

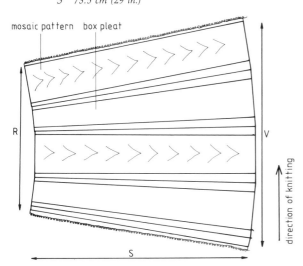

# WEDDING DRESS

## (*Chapter 8, Fig. 86*)

### UNDER-DRESS

The bodice and the set-in sleeves are fitted; the skirt is a simple 'A' line. Calculate the skirt measurements using the same principle as the braid dress (*Fig. 107*).

### OVERSKIRT AND CAPE

The overskirt and cape are knitted in tuck and slip stitch using thick and thin yarn (*Chapter 8*). The panels have a curved base. There are three ways of working out how many stitches need to be increased to reproduce the curve.

1 The simplest way of knitting a curve is to draw a panel onto the charting device and follow this.

2 If you do not have a charting device then draw out the shape on proportional graph paper which is now available (see p. 155 for details). This will give a guide to the number of increases and the number of stitches in those increases in a visual way.

3 The third method of calculation is to use the magic formula recommended by Kathleen Kinder in *Machine Knitting: The Technique of Knitweave* (see p. 153).

The cape and the overskirt (*Fig. 107*), knitted in tuck and slip stitch, use the same panel shape. They differ only in the length. For the overskirt knit 8 panels as follows: 2 each of 4, 5 and 6, plus one each of 3 (centre front) and 7 (centre back). Suggested length of overskirt panels: shortest panel (panel pattern 3) = 54 cm (21 in.), then increase the length of each panel pattern by 10.2 cm (4 in.). The overskirt has a centre panel at the back and front. The cape has two matching panels at the centre front and a long centre panel at the back. For the cape, knit 7 panels as follows: 2 each of 1, 2 and 3 plus one of panel 4 (centre back). Thus the cape has two matching panels at the centre front and a long centre panel at the back. Suggested length of cape panels: shortest panels (panel pattern 1) = 33.2 cm (13 in.), then increase the length of each panel pattern by 10.2 cm (4 in.).

147

# MOSAIC PLEATED SKIRT

## (*Chapter 9, Fig. 96*)

Use the details given in Chapter 9 for calculating the skirt length. To calculate the number of pleats required, measure the width of the straight (pattern) panel. The width is then divided into the hip measurement to give the number of pleats which need to be knitted. The diagram in Fig. 108 shows the skirt as it will appear on the machine.

The pattern is a four-stitch repeat. Mark it out with double-row marking as in the original design and repeat across the card. Brother electronic machine owners need only select a four-stitch-wide section of the mylar sheet and programme as appropriate.

Work the mosaic pattern in section 4 of the box pleat using PP29.

# MOCK PLEATED DRESS

## (*Chapter 9, Fig. 96*)

The skirt is worked using the mylar sheet in Fig. 91. The yarn is changed to a different thickness in the straight sections to produce the mock pleats. The top is shorter than the skirt and will not use the full width of the pattern (*Fig. 109*).

The same mylar sheet can be used but there will be more rows in each straight section. The design can be redrawn to allow for the ten straight rows used in the skirt. Alternatively use the ridge pattern with ten straight rows between each half wedge.

*109 Mock-pleated dress. Note: these pieces are knitted sideways.*

| Skirt | | Bodice | |
|---|---|---|---|
| R | 43.5 cm (17 in.) | M | 46 cm (18 in.) |
| S | 73.5 cm (29 in.) | R | 43.5 cm (17 in.) |
| b | R + wedge shaping | W | 25.5 cm (10 in.) |
| | | g | 18 cm (7 in.) |

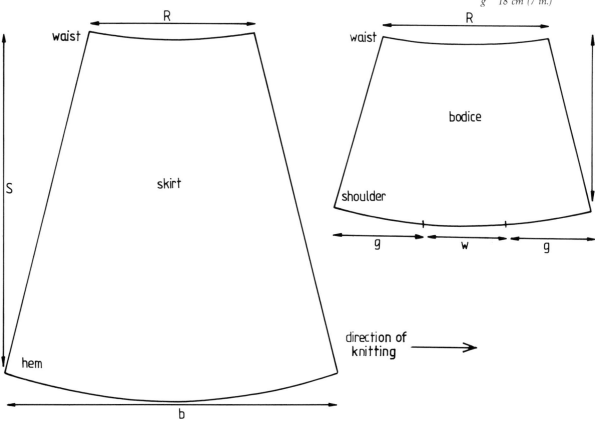

# PATTERN DETAILS

**Tops, dresses and skirts**

## Reducing stitches along a row

1 Calculate the number of stitches to be reduced in the row.

2 Select this number evenly across the needlebed. Transfer the selected stitches to adjacent needles using a lace carriage if you have a Brother machine; otherwise by hand. Return the empty needles to non-working position. Knit one row. Strip off with waste yarn.

## Cuffs, welts, bands and neckbands

A simple way of knitting welts and cuffs whether you own a ribber or not is to knit a stocking stitch hem. It is a method which I use in preference to the mock rib recommended in most of the manuals. To keep the hems stable add a strand of fine yarn to the main yarn and knit at main tension.

A decision has to be made as to how many stitches are required for the hem, as it is knitted before the garment is attached. Using this method the finishing process is almost complete when you take the garment off the machine.

Present the garment to the machine with the centre of the piece to the centre of the needlebed. Allow the centre section of the garment to curve about 4–5 cm ($1\frac{1}{2}$–2 in.) below the needlebed. The drop gives an allowance which is used up as the garment is picked up onto the needles. Where the outer edges of the garment rest on the needlebed indicates the number of stitches to be cast on for the relevant band.

The method is not very scientific but it does work; use it for neckbands, cuffs and welts. If a more precise calculation is preferred then refer to the many informative books by Kathleen Kinder, Mary Weaver and *To and Fro* magazine which cover the problem in great detail.

# KNITTING INSTRUCTIONS

**Welt, cuff, neckband, etc.**

1 Cast on in WY over the required number of needles. Knit a few rows. Change to MY.

2 Knit the required number of rows, a foldline and the second half of the hem.

3 Pick up the first row knitted in MY. Knit 1 row.

4 Place appropriate section of garment onto machine with right side facing hem. Pick up one full stitch along the edge to stabilize the join. Knit 1 row TD8 then 1 row TD10. Cast off.

The cast-off depends entirely on which part of the garment is being finished. Cuffs must have enough stretch to slip over the hand; a crew neck must fit over the head. To obtain a loose cast-off, lift up the ribber bed which is set to H, select every alternate needle on the ribber, connect the ribber arm and knit one row. Drop the loops formed on the ribber and cast off as normal.

If you do not own a ribber then the Passap method of wrapping the yarn around the needle twice – once round the shaft, once inside the latch – before casting off gives the correct amount of flexibility.

*Punchcard pattern sheet 8*

43E

48

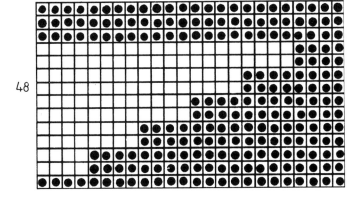

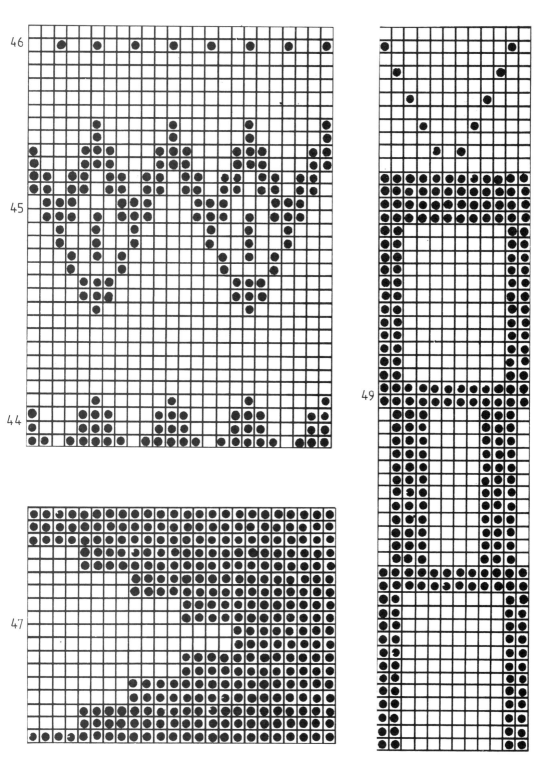

# Further reading

**Australian Machine Knitters Magazine**
68 Middleton Street
Watsonia 3087
Australia
(Published quarterly)

**Modern Machine Knitting**
Modern Knitting Ltd
Kingston on Thames
(Published monthly)

**To and Fro Postal Knitting Club**
321 Ashley Road
Parkstone
Poole
Dorset
BH14 0AP

**Armitage, Kate**
*Card 3* (MSM Publications, Bournemouth, 1985)

**Bradley, Sue**
*Stitches in Time* (Orbis, London, 1986)

**Brooks, Sara**
*Garment Shaping Electronically* (Sara Brooks, Washington, USA, 1982)

**Kinder, Kathleen**
*A Resource Book for Machine Knitters* (1979)
*A Second Resource Book for Machine Knitters* (1980)
*A Resource Book Pattern Supplement* (1983)
*The Machine Knitter's Book of the Ribber* Volumes 1 and 2 (1984 and 1985)
*Mosaic Floatless Fair Isle* (1987)
(the above from Valley View, Station Road, Giggleswick, Settle, North Yorkshire)
*Techniques in Machine Knitting* (Batsford, 1983)
*Machine Knitting: The Technique of Knitweave* (Batsford, 1987)

**Lewis, Susanna and Weissman, Julia**
*A Machine Knitter's Guide to Creating Fabrics* (Lark Books, 1986)

**McGregor, Sheila**
*The Complete Book of Traditional Fair Isle Knitting* (Batsford, 1981)

**O'Connor, Kaori**
*Creative Dressing* (Routledge & Kegan Paul, London, 1980)

**Walker, Barbara**
*A Treasury of Knitting Patterns* (Scribners and Sons, New York, 1968)
*A Second Treasury of Knitting Patterns* (Scribners and Sons, New York, 1970)
*Charted Knitting Designs, A Third Treasury of Knitting Patterns*, (Scribners and Sons, New York, 1972)

**Weaver, Mary**
*The Ribbing Attachment Part 1* (1974)
*The Ribbing Attachment Part 2* (1976)
*Single Bed Technology* (1979)
(from 8 Craybrooke Road, Sidcup, Kent DA4 9HJ)

# Appendix

# Yarn and sundries suppliers

## UK

**Bedford Sewing and Knitting Machines Ltd**
13 Lime Street
Bedford MK40 1LD
*Machines, accessories, yarn, books and magazines*

**British Mohair Spinners Ltd**
PO Box 58, Midland Mills
Valley Road, Bradford
West Yorkshire BD1 4RL
*Mohair yarn*

**The Flamingo Wool Shop**
118 Sunbridge Road
Bradford BD1 2NE
*Machines, accessories, yarn, books and magazines*

**Jamieson and Smith Ltd**
90 North Road
Lerwick
Shetland Isle ZE1 0PQ
*Shetland yarn only*

**Metropolitan Sewing Machines**
321 Ashley Road
Parkstone, Poole
Dorset BH14 0AP
*Machines, accessories, yarn, books and magazines*

**Texere Yarns**
College Mill
Barkerend Road
Bradford BD3 9AQ
*Yarns both natural and man-made*

**The Textile Bookshop**
Tynwald Mills
St John's
Isle of Man
*Proportional graph paper available by mail order; callers by appointment only*

**Worth Knitting**
Clifton Hill, Pudsey
West Yorkshire
*Machines, accessories, yarn, books and magazines*

## SUNDRIES

**R.L. & C.M. Bond**
Town Street
Farsley, Pudsey
West Yorkshire
*Beads, braids, buttons, sewing thread, sequins, beaded motifs, etc.*

## USA

**Cardinal**
1920 Vermillion Road
PO Box 5872
Brownsville
Texas 78520

**Frances Collins**
Importer (Bramwell Yarns)
PO Box 8244
Midland
TX 79708

**Joseph Galler Inc.**
27 West 20th Street
New York
NY 10011

**School Products Co. Inc.**
1201 Broadway
New York
NY 10001

**Scott's Woolen Mill Inc.**
528 Jefferson Ave.
PO Box 1204
Bristol
PA 19007

## Australia

**Bendigo Woollen Mills**
PO Box 119
Kangaroo Flat
Victoria 3555
Australia

**Regent Knitwear**
138–140 Regent Street
Redfern 2016

**'Tessa B' Knits**
98A Norma Road
Myaree 6154
Western Australia

**Taxtor Trading Co.**
9 Brighton Street
Richmond 3121

# Index